Wake up to experience the most amazing

gift the Universe has bestowed

upon You!

The highest purpose of life —

is to experience your Soul!

Immerse in the ocean of bliss within you.

Quiet your hungry mind,

let your happy soul shine!

Happy Soul.
Hungry Mind.

A modern-day parable about Spirituality

Volume 1 — Tribulations

First Edition

RAVI GOPALDAS KATHURIA

HappySoulHungryMind.com

Published by SeemaCorp
Copyright © 2018 by Ravi Gopaldas Kathuria
ISBN: 978-0-9821475-5-9
Version: 001 – June 14, 2018
First Edition Name (Released November 2018):
    Happy Soul. Hungry Mind. Volume 1

Dedicated to my dear parents,

Gopaldas and Dropadi Kathuria,

to my darling wife,

Seema,

and our loving sons, Amrit and Aayush.

And, to our dear friend, Murli,

who valiantly fought cancer for thirteen years.

Contents

Introduction

Happiness! We all want it, but we fail to understand it. You cannot achieve what you do not understand. We have all the comforts of modern life, yet anxiety and stress steal our happiness every day.

Your mind can be your biggest friend or your worst enemy. Are you the slave or the master of your mind? *The secrets to success and happiness lie within your mind.* Learn to master your mind. This modern-day parable offers you practical ways to be happier. Learn how to be happier and live a glorious life!

Throughout history, people have sought answers for life's important questions: What is the ultimate purpose of our lives? Is there a difference between religion and spirituality? And, the most debated questions: What is God? Did God create man or did man create God? Why we cannot "see" God?

The answers to these questions have been mysterious and misleading. This book provides clear and logical answers. If people appreciate and adopt these answers, it will propel human evolution and change the course of human history for the next ten thousand years!

This emotion and humor-filled parable is easy and fun to read. Its purpose is to make spirituality simple to understand for everyone and present it in a modern manner. This book reveals the highest *spiritual gems* free of religious beliefs. These gems can uplift your life in ways you cannot imagine!

This book does not ask for blind faith. Challenge every gem and test it for yourself. *Truth does not need a leap of faith.*

Imagine your mother gives you a valuable and beautiful gift wrapped in a box. You play with the colorful wrapping paper but never open the box. You do not enjoy the gift even though it is all yours.

That is what you are doing with your life. You are spending all your time focused outside on the material world, ignoring the magnificent spiritual world within you. Do not spend all your time on the wrapping paper. *Open the box.*

Read this book to truly understand happiness. All the best to you on the most important mission of your life!

Chapter 1: Pain

The journey of life is as mysterious and fascinating as anyone can imagine. Most of the time it moves like a slow river, meandering its way, giving no indication about the approaching thunderous waterfall.

People come into our lives, some stay for a long time, others only for a fleeting moment. Most of our interactions disappear into the waves of time with little impact. Some change the course of our lives. The river of life flows again with full gusto toward its destination.

It was Saturday morning. As Rishi Rupani enjoyed the view of the Las Vegas strip from the 57th-floor penthouse suite he heard a knock. He glanced at his attractive gold bezel watch. It showed 7:30 AM. Rishi walked to open the door.

Travis Hensley stood at the door. Rishi extended his hand and with a warm smile welcomed him in.

"Right on time," said Rishi, as they walked in.

Travis turned to Rishi. "Least I could do after my behavior last night." Rishi did not comment and continued walking.

"Wow, nice penthouse," said Travis. "Elegant."

"Thanks." Rishi stopped by the sofa.

"Must cost a bundle," said Travis.

"A perk of the four large conferences a year we do." Rishi smiled. He was a senior vice president for a Houston, Texas, based company, Hinteq. In his late-forties, Rishi immigrated from India in his early twenties to pursue higher education.

"Cool!" Travis looked around. Floor to ceiling glass windows spanned the west side of the two-story suite, lined with beige sheer curtains. Travis walked to the windows. The curtains were drawn but allowed enough light to come in.

"Come, have a seat," said Rishi.

Travis headed toward the two English colonial chairs.

"We'll be more comfortable here." Rishi pointed to one of the two large maroon fabric sofas facing each other.

Travis made himself comfortable pushing aside several of the red velvet pillows embroidered with soft golden edges. "Four conferences, that's a lot."

"You bet," said Rishi raising his black, well-groomed eyebrows. "Lot of hard work, we get a large attendance. Can I get you something? We have juices, coffee, fruits, cereal bars."

"No, thanks, I had a big breakfast after my jog."

"Okay, maybe later." Rishi sat down on the opposite sofa.

"Thanks for spending time with me today," said Travis.

"Oh, absolutely. I had no plans, I was just going to unwind from the conference," said Rishi. "What about you?"

"It's a busy weekend. Meeting with the team in the afternoon and all day tomorrow," said Travis. He was the CEO of Travisto, a startup company developing mobile software apps.

"How are the preparations for next week?" asked Rishi.

"We decided to revise the whole investor presentation, so it's taking a lot of time and effort," said Travis.

"By the way, I like the name Travisto," said Rishi.

Travis smiled. "It means a person who relies on intuition to make decisions. Hate to admit it, but my Mom suggested it."

Rishi laughed. "Very good."

Travis glanced away. "I apologize for last night."

"Uh…." Rishi pressed his lips. "I didn't like the way you lost your temper at the waitress. I've never seen you behave that way. Jake and I were embarrassed."

"I'm sorry," said Travis. "I shouldn't have been rude. I'm sorry to embarrass you in front of your colleague."

"It's okay, I spoke to Jake later, he's fine… but what you did driving me back…."

Travis cringed.

Rishi widened his eyes. "You could've put us in harm's way."

"I shouldn't have chased after that SUV." Travis touched his chest with both hands. "I'm truly sorry."

"I was scared."

"I'm really sorry." Travis drooped.

"It's okay, let's move on," said Rishi.

"I was afraid you might change your mind about meeting me," said Travis as he eyed Rishi carefully.

Rishi shook his head. "Noooo, I wouldn't do that." He tapped the sofa. "You're a friend. We barely had time to talk last night. I've missed you. Five years is a long time."

"Seems longer," said Travis. "I'm sorry I haven't been in touch after I left Ixsor. I felt terrible I bolted on you close to that big deadline. I was afraid you'd always hate me."

Rishi waved his hand. "I'd never hate you. I knew how important it was for you to start a company."

"It was. I didn't want the angel investor in San Jose to walk away." Travis exhaled. "And, it's been non-stop once I got there. I just didn't have the time —"

"No worries," interjected Rishi. "So, what's happening? You said you wanted to discuss something important. You need my advice on Travisto?"

"I… I…." Travis took a deep breath. "Life's become a big challenge."

"Why?" asked Rishi.

Travis eyed Rishi slowly, his energy falling. "Been wanting… needing to talk to someone." Travis's eyes still meandering, he glanced at the curved, wrought iron staircase leading upstairs on the south end of the suite. "Seeing your conference picture in the lobby yesterday was a sign."

Rishi looked on perplexed.

Travis continued, "I hesitated at first to come see you —"

Rishi interjected with a thumbs up. "I'm glad you sought me out. When I saw you I couldn't believe my eyes."

Travis looked down. "You were always there for me when we worked together… when I worked for you," said Travis.

"Well…," said Rishi.

"You were there for everyone else too," said Travis.

Rishi wagged his finger with a smile. "Flattery isn't going to get you anywhere."

"I'm serious," said Travis softly. "Ixsor would've fired me if you hadn't saved my back."

"Well, I just appreciated the great software programmer that lurked behind —"

"My bad attitude?"

Rishi shook his head. "You're the consummate engineer. Sometimes, how you say things can be —"

"Offensive?" said Travis.

"Well, abrupt," said Rishi.

"Without your mentoring... I wouldn't be where I am today." Travis shook his head slowly. "No chance." His eyes meandered, "I never had a boss or a teacher like you."

"I enjoyed working with you," said Rishi. "It was always fun and stimulating."

"You cared about me... never had a friend like you... I... I trust you... more than anyone else," said Travis. "I'm serious."

Rishi stiffened. He had never seen Travis in such a listless mood.

"Life's become... a burden." Travis pushed aside his light brown hair from his forehead, looked to the side with his light grey eyes, and breathed slowly.

"A burden? Has work become overwhelming?" asked Rishi.

Travis did not answer, his eyes glazed in the direction of the two-story mahogany bookshelves adorning the wall behind the staircase. The bookshelves created an impressive backdrop, but they barely registered with Travis.

Rishi sat up straighter. He began to lean forward when Travis turned to him. "My son died."

All of Las Vegas went silent. Rishi froze in his seat. He put his fist to his mouth. "Oh, my God, Travis! I'm so sorry."

"My child," Travis's face reflected deep pain, "died."

Forcing himself to fight his shock, Rishi took his hand off. "When... how?"

Travis did not respond, doing his best to control his emotions. He failed. A stream of tears ran down his cheek.

Rishi stood up and walked around the coffee table to sit beside Travis. He gently patted Travis on the back. "I'm so sorry, Travis." Rishi's eyes filled up. "Nathan —"

"He was only seven," said Travis.

"...When?" Rishi could barely speak.

"Nine months ago. I just can't believe it. Don't wanna believe it. I just don't." Tears rolled down Travis's cheeks.

Rishi put his arm around Travis's back and squeezed his shoulder. He sat quietly. After a few moments that seemed like an eternity, he got up, walked to the bar, picked a crystal glass and filled it with ice and water. Travis took a sip. Rishi sat back down on his sofa, not sure what to say next.

Travis took a few moments and regained some of his composure. He finished off the water. "Thanks."

"I can remember him playing in my arms," said Rishi. "He was so cute and lively."

Travis nodded slowly. "He loved soccer... could score a goal with just a flick of his foot. I loved watching him."

Rishi wanted to ask how it had happened but did not want to cause more pain.

"We came back from soccer practice one evening," said Travis, "Nathan had a fever. Cindi and I put him to bed early, but by midnight, his temperature had risen to 103. We took him to the children's hospital."

Rishi listened quietly.

"In the morning, they told us they were moving him to the intensive care unit. We couldn't understand why."

"Then?" asked Rishi.

"The doctors explained later he had a swelling in his brain. The tests showed a viral infection, likely due to a mosquito."

"Viral infection — in the brain?"

"Yup, most people don't get affected, but somehow in Nathan's case the virus reached his brain."

"Why couldn't they treat him?" asked Rishi.

"One-in-a-hundred-thousand-case. Viruses rarely are able to infect the brain. He was in the ICU for three days. Finally, they said his body just couldn't fight anymore. My little son was gone." Travis choked up. "In four short days, he'd gone from a healthy, cheerful kid to completely frail and dead. We didn't know what had hit us. Cindi, I, we couldn't think straight." Travis shook his head. "Still can't believe it."

"How's Cindi?" asked Rishi.

"Better than me," said Travis. "She's stronger. He'd wear this sleeveless soccer jersey. I'd tell him, 'Nathan, you don't have muscles, why are you wearing sleeveless.' He'd immediately flex his arm. 'No Dad, I have muscles, see, see.' God, I miss him." Travis clamped his fists.

Rishi looked around the room, searching for something to say. He did not have the words.

Travis closed his eyes. "Suffocating… I feel like exploding." Travis held his head. He opened his eyes. "Cindi and I've been to grief counselors, they're not of much help. They ask us to describe what happened and it forces us to relive those moments. We stopped seeing them."

That is not good, thought Rishi.

"We're zombies when we're home, nothing to say."

"You both need to talk to someone. It's important to talk."

"Cindi talks to her friends. She's doing a lot better, slowly coming around. She's recovered… somewhat, I'm… sinking."

"Why?" asked Rishi with a worried look.

"No one to talk to. I don't want to talk to my parents. I can't talk about it at work, and you know I don't have many friends. You were my friend, used talk to me about life, spirituality… and peace… I want to sleep peacefully for one night." Travis closed his eyes. "Want to sleep for one freaking night."

Travis slumped his head into the sofa. "So exhausted... so tired."

Rishi's eye moistened, tears running down his cheeks. He could not bear to see Travis in such a state.

Travis looked up at Rishi and saw him looking lost. "You've got to help me, Rishi. Can you help me?"

Chapter 2: Healing

Rishi was susceptible to other people's pain and emotions. Whenever he would read the headlines of a tragedy, he would not read the story because it would affect his emotional being. He was overwhelmed but realized Travis needed him.

Travis pursed his lips. "I can be fine for days, caught up in work, then it hits hard again. I figured with time I'd feel better, I'm not... I don't wanna live anymore."

"Don't say that. Never ever say that, ever!"

"I don't know what to do...." Travis breathed loudly as if he could not find oxygen.

"I'd love to help you. God, I'd love to help you." Rishi looked away. "But I'm not your guy. I don't talk to people who are grieving. I don't know how to." He had a helpless look.

"Yeah, you do," said Travis, "your admin... Kathy, her husband died."

"That was different, Kathy had been expecting it. It was a relief for her and her husband whose suffering ended. She had kids and grandkids. I just comforted her a bit."

"You did more than that. No other boss would've done that much. I remember you consoling her often."

"I must've been stronger then... I've become vulnerable...." Rishi closed his eyes. "Travis, I'm stunned about Nathan... it's hit me hard. I played with Nathan, carried him around. I can almost feel him in my arms." He opened his moist eyes. "I wish I could help, but I'm just not capable." Rishi shook his head slowly and looked away.

"You're fully capable." Travis leaned in. "You have a good heart. Only one who can talk to me — please." He pressed his palms together. "I know I haven't been in touch and I'm really sorry for not staying in touch, but you... you are my only...."

Rishi could not deny Travis. He did not want him to plead anymore. "Okay." Rishi gestured gently with his hands. "I'll talk to you." He collected himself. "Where do you want to start, what do you want to discuss — your feelings, your emotions?"

"No." Travis looked resolute. "Spirituality."

Rishi looked surprised. "Now?"

"Why not?" said Travis. "You're thinking we're in Las Vegas."

"No, no, why spirituality...," said Rishi.

"I want to have the kind of discussions we used to have."

"Our spiritual discussions? You sure?" asked Rishi.

"You're thinking I didn't pay attention back then."

"No." Rishi looked circumspect. "Is this the right time?"

"It is," said Travis. "I used to brush you aside, make smart remarks, but it used to bring me peace. It really used to. I remember some of what you used to say, but I need to hear it again." Travis touched the side of his ear.

"I used to enjoy discussing spirituality with you, but...."

"You repeated it so many times," said Travis, "spirituality makes you calm and peaceful. I just want to feel calm."

Rishi squirmed. "Spiritual discussions are about becoming healthy over a period of time. It's not about helping a patient in the emergency room. You need immediate help, not a discussion about becoming healthy over the long term."

"I need immediate help, but I really need long-term help. I can't sweep this away, something in me is dying."

As Rishi pondered, Travis said, "You used to say spirituality helps us at the deepest levels, that's what I need. I'm done with people telling me God loved Nathan and that's why he had to go. What BS!" Scorn on his face, Travis said, "One more person says that I'll punch them in the face." He closed his eyes. "I don't know anyone else… please, only you can take me to peace."

All right, Rishi thought to himself, when Travis said, "I was in a terrible mood yesterday. During a break, I ventured out to take a phone call, and ended up in the roller coaster area."

Rishi listened.

"I saw a young boy about Nathan's age. He was pulling his father's hand to go on the roller coaster. It tore my heart. Nathan would pull me just like that." Travis clinched his fist tight and ground his teeth. "I don't know why God did this to me. I just hate it. I hate God!" His breathing became heavier and his face red. "Why did God have to do this to little Nathan? Nathan never did anything bad. My poor baby, he was such a sweet kid. How could God kill him?"

Rishi shook his head vigorously.

"Then who did?" Travis looked piercingly.

Rishi struggled. "Travis… would you do me a favor?"

Travis did not answer and looked away.

Rishi waited. "Travis, please… would you do me a favor?"

Travis shrugged. "Okay… whatever."

Rishi spoke in a calm and reassuring tone. "Please, would you close your eyes… and take three deep breaths."

Travis was too agitated. He continued to look away.

Rishi watched Travis's pain and felt the entire room constricting. Rishi did not say anything, the silence deafening.

After a few moments, Travis turned his head toward Rishi and followed his suggestion. He shut his eyes.

As gently as he could, Rishi said, "Breathe…," after a few seconds, Rishi repeated, "breathe… breathe…." Rishi did not say anything else, just watched Travis with closed eyes continue to breathe. Several moments passed, Travis opened his eyes.

Rishi took a deep breath himself and then walked over to Travis. "May I touch you?"

Travis nodded his head slightly in approval.

Rishi touched the space between Travis's eyebrows with his right thumb. Travis lowered his eyelids. Rishi put his palm over Travis's eyes and stood quietly. He could hear Travis breathe. Next, he touched Travis on the top of his head. He applied a slight pressure with his four fingers, feeling Travis's thick hair.

Travis kept his eyes closed as his breathing slowed. Rishi sat down next to Travis and patted his back a couple of times. Travis's breathing slowed further. Rishi waited silently a few moments until Travis calmed down, and then walked back to his seat.

Travis felt a sense of calm as if he had finally found someone who could shelter him from the terrible reality, to whom he could surrender.

Rishi sat down on his sofa. Travis looked at Rishi in anticipation, hungry for relief, not knowing what to expect.

"There are people who are looking for a quick weight loss and those who are looking for endurance training," said Rishi.

Travis looked squarely at Rishi. With conviction, he said, "I'm not looking for a quick fix. I want to change my life."

"I'm happy to talk about spirituality, I don't get many takers." Rishi decided to throw in some humor. "Even my own wife doesn't want to talk spirituality with me. Nothing is a better use of my time. Nothing more beneficial for you — and me."

"I need spiritual progress." Travis exhaled. "You've always said there's more to life than our current existence. You used to ask me, 'Are you as happy and content as you can be.' I used to think yes, of course, but now I've realized, I was happy, busy with life, but was I content? No? I don't think I even know what it means to be content."

Rishi caressed his forehead.

Travis lowered his eyes. "Is there a meaning to my life?"

There is infinitely more to life than your current existence. Experience it.

Are you as blissful and content as you can be?

Is there a meaning to your life?

"Travis, I can't fathom what you've gone through, but if you walk on the path of spirituality, you'll develop a much better ability to handle life. Spirituality will create a protective layer. You'll become peaceful, and life won't ever be such a bone-crushing burden."

"Exactly what I need," said Travis lifting his chin. "Wish I'd called you nine months ago... maybe I wasn't ready then. Seeing you is such a relief, such a lucky break. But, it's not just Nathan. Travisto has been a huge challenge too. Five years into it and I'm still not there. It's as if my whole life has become so heavy. That's what I need help in, I want to breathe."

Rishi put his fist below his chin in thought. "Let's set expectations. I can't fix you overnight, it'll take time."

"I know it's not gonna happen overnight."

"Forget overnight, this path could take years, even an entire lifetime. This journey is only for the most serious. Even I'm not sure if I'm committed enough to my own spiritual journey."

"I'm not going to let you back out, buddy. I'm living in hell." The pain on Travis's face resurfaced.

Rishi shifted uncomfortably. "Travis, I need to help you calm down before we can talk spirituality, otherwise, you won't… your emotions are driving you crazy."

Travis's nostrils flared. "My emotions aren't driving me crazy, Nathan's death is driving me crazy."

Rishi moved his feet on the rug back and forth. "Nathan's death affected Cindi and you. Then… why's Cindi handling it better?"

Travis ruffled his hair. "Because she…."

"Because her emotions are in control," said Rishi. "She's handling it better, and more importantly, is suffering less than you."

Travis became quiet.

"Your mind's driving you crazy, hers is not. At least, not as much as yours."

"I'm missing him more." Travis's nostrils flared again like a bull ready for a fight.

"Your mind is hungering for him." Rishi pointed a finger at Travis, firm in his voice. "You're playing Nathan's video in your mind over and over again. When you see a kid in the roll-er coaster area, you play the Nathan video, and keep playing it until you're so frustrated you're ready to run over people with your car at the slightest provocation."

"How can I... how can I not remember him? ...Forget my son?" A painful look replaced the flaring nostrils. "How can I insult his memory?"

Rishi interlocked his fingers. "Travis," he said in an assur-ing tone, "you're not insulting his memory. Instead, what you're doing is using his memory to torture yourself."

Travis had no comeback.

"In a way, you like that sadistic pain." Rishi lifted his palms slightly. "I'm not picking on you. Our minds are horrible in that way. When we go through a deep loss, our mind sucks us into an endless whirlpool of sadness, regret, guilt, blame, anger, what-ifs, could-haves, and should-haves. Do you feel more pain because you feel guilty you didn't spend time with him?"

Travis did not answer refusing to make eye contact.

Rishi waited.

"I don't know... maybe," said Travis under his breath.

"If there's guilt, stop it. Cease the guilt. Doesn't matter what we lose, a loved one, money, job, reputation, whatever, our mind takes us through the wash-and-rinse cycle endlessly."

Travis closed his fist. "How do we stop the darn thing?"

"By accepting the fact."

Travis slumped and let his eyelids drop. He put one arm over his head, arching it so it touched the back of the sofa.

"Please accept the fact," said Rishi as comfortingly as he could.

Travis opened his eyes and put his arm down. He pressed his lips.

"Release the anger," Rishi unfurled his fingers, "let it release."

Travis stood up and paced along the windows.

A thought crossed Rishi's mind about walking up to Travis and squeezing his shoulders. He decided against it, recognizing Travis may need some time.

Walking back and forth, stopping several times, Travis looked down, not once looking out the windows. Finally, he said, "May I have some more water."

"Sure." Rishi sprung up. Travis walked over to the bar with Rishi. Travis stood by the large granite island with brown leather bar stools underneath. Travis drank some water. They refilled the glass and walked back to the sofas.

"I don't know how to let go," said Travis as they sat down.

"Start by forgiving yourself, God, fate… whatever else."

"How can I forgive God?" Travis had a puzzled look. "Me, forgive God?"

"The emphasis is not on God, it's on forgive." Rishi looked intently. "Your mind will hound you until you forgive. In your case it's God, or really that mosquito," said Rishi, afraid he might be belittling Nathan's death. "It doesn't matter whom you forgive, but you must. Only when you forgive, will you let go. And, forgive yourself — release the guilt. Only when you let go, will you accept it."

Travis looked away. "Why this freaking world —"

"Why is this world this way?"

Travis nodded, his lips pursed.

"Wish I knew," said Rishi shaking his head, "why there are so many sorrows, so much pain in this world."

"Horrrrrible," said Travis in a deep guttural voice.

"It is," said Rishi, "but we must accept it. It is what it is."

"So, that's where the saying comes from," said Travis in a sarcastic tone.

Rishi nodded slightly. "Your mind needs to find peace. Using Nathan's memories to torture yourself is insulting his memory. Use his memory to make yourself happy." Rishi stretched his palms out. "Can you please repeat after me, Nathan, I bless you, wherever you are, I bless you."

Travis squinted, unsure, and then followed the instruction in a slow, serious voice. "Nathan I bless you, wherever you are."

Rishi continued, "Wherever you are I love you. Nathan, thank you for spending time with us. Thank you, buddy. Thank you, Nathan."

"Thank you, buddy, thank you, Nathan," said Travis. "Thank you, cutie Nathan." Travis's eyes welled up.

Rishi's eyes welled up too. He wiped the tears. "Please say, I forgive myself. I free myself from any guilt."

Travis took a deep breath. "Just like that?"

"Yes, please say, I free myself of guilt."

"I free myself of guilt," said Travis out of respect for Rishi, not buying into the utterances. Rishi sensed the skepticism.

"Our mind works at the conscious level and many layers of the subconscious," said Rishi. "These statements, even if you don't believe in them at the conscious levels, will leave their mark at the subconscious level. I promise you, if you repeat, I free myself of guilt, a thousand times, your mind will believe it, and you'll feel better. Can you say it a couple more times?"

"I free myself of guilt. I'm free... I free myself of guilt."

"Thank you," said Rishi. "I can't snap my fingers and take your grief away in a day. I can only hope to take the sting out of your pain. By repeating these sentences, as superficial as they may seem, hopefully, your pain will break, just as a fever breaks. Can you say again, I love you, Nathan, I bless you wherever you are."

"I love you, Nathan." Travis paused. "I bless you wherever you are." Travis took a deep breath. "I bless you, Nathan."

"And can you ask Cindi to say the same?"

"I will." Travis nodded.

Rishi gave Travis some time to breathe. Travis's breathing slowed. He drank a sip of water.

"How are you feeling," asked Rishi.

Travis looked up. "I feel… better… at least better than yesterday. Talking to you has helped me… thank you."

"Sure," said Rishi, relieved a bit.

"Are we going to discuss spirituality?" asked Travis.

"Yes, we are," said Rishi with a slight smile intrigued by Travis's persistence. He raised his finger. "There's one issue — I might fail to help you. I have too many shortcomings."

"I don't care about that. No way out for you, brother."

Rishi sighed. "I'm struggling in so many ways. I'm still learning, I haven't reached my destination."

"You're all I got," said Travis gazing intently at Rishi.

Rishi could no longer dismiss Travis's urgings. "I'll help you as best as I can."

"That's all I ask," said Travis relaxing.

"We won't be able to have a successful discussion if…," Rishi caressed his forehead, "we need to, if possible… take your mind off of Nathan so you can focus on our discussion. So, I'm going to do my best not to bring up…"

Travis nodded gently. "Okay… it'll be difficult but I won't bring it up either."

"All right," said Rishi relaxing a little. "Let's discuss life's most important questions."

Travis gave a firm nod.

"Before we begin, why don't you take a minute to freshen up? Some coffee or juice?"

"Coffee would be great." Travis stood up.

"Restroom is behind the bar," said Rishi pointing the way.

Travis washed his face, wiping away the sticky tears. He brushed his hair, tucked his white polo t-shirt in his brown khaki pants. After wiping the granite around the glass sink bowl with several Kleenex tissues, he walked back to the sitting area. Instead of sitting down, he walked to the windows, parted the curtains and looked out at the mountains behind the Las Vegas strip and its line of casinos.

"Would you like to sit out on the balcony?" asked Rishi while pouring Travis's coffee.

"No, it's comfortable in here," said Travis looking out at the wrought iron patio furniture outside.

"Okay." Rishi walked back, placed the cup of coffee on the coffee table, and placed a coaster underneath the hot cup. Standing next to the window Travis quickly answered a few emails and text messages on his phone.

As Travis walked back, Rishi said, "I'm going to get comfortable and take my shoes off. My feet like to breathe and I might cross my legs on the sofa. You're welcome to do so too."

"I'll leave them on, thanks for the coffee."

Rishi took his shoes and socks off and carried them off the beautiful large silk rug. Dressed in light cream khaki pants and a starched, light orange, half-sleeved, designer shirt, with dark brown buttons, Rishi looked warm and hospitable.

Sitting back down Rishi moved his feet back and forth on the rug, feeling its silky smooth texture. He relished the feeling.

His face relaxed and his hazel colored, light brown eyes glimmered in the light from the windows. On his wheatish complexion face, the eyes had a hypnotic draw. In his late-forties, Rishi had a large forehead due to a receding hairline. His large forehead, a perfectly styled short haircut, and his light eyes blended together to give Rishi a distinctive executive look.

Travis reached for the red ceramic cup and took a slow sip of the coffee. Rishi was eager for the discussion but wondered if Travis was in the right frame of mind. Rishi worried if he could help Travis or would the discussion stir up more emotions.

Chapter 3: Hungry Mind

"Ready?" asked Rishi, ascertaining Travis's emotional state.

Travis gave a firm nod. "More than ready… I've forgotten a lot, I wanna let it sink in deep this time."

Rishi felt encouraged. "Challenge as you used to. You won't believe how much I liked our debates. It used to help me distill my thinking."

"Always happy to challenge," said Travis. "You used to say, 'There's lot more to life than the life we're living,' and boy do I need to figure that out."

"We all do — especially me," said Rishi.

"Can we save all the attention for me?" said Travis in a playful tone.

"Yes, sir!" Rishi smiled, happy Travis was engaging. "To discuss spirituality we first need to understand the mind."

"Are brain and mind the same?" asked Travis.

"No, brain is the hardware, mind is the software and data. Mind is your thoughts, emotions, and feelings. Based on your memories, experiences, habits, desires, and actions the mind develops its unique personality."

> *Brain is the hardware. Mind is the software and data. The mind generates thoughts, emotions and feelings.*

"Isn't the heart the seat of emotions?" asked Travis.

"No, emotions first arise in the mind, and then affect different organs. If it's love or sadness, you'll feel it in the heart or chest. Anxiety and fear, you'll feel in the stomach, and so on."

"Okay," said Travis.

"From the moment we're born," Rishi touched his chest, "every one of us is looking for happiness."

"I certainly am," said Travis.

"Those who are distraught are even willing to end their lives, that's the hold happiness has on us."

Travis turned sober.

"Our minds are restless and hungry," said Rishi. "Our eternally hungry minds rob us of our internal peace. It's the greatest irony of life —"

Our minds are restless and hungry.

"What?" asked Travis.

"Our pursuit of temporary happiness steals our permanent happiness," said Rishi. "It's the biggest blunder of our lives."

Travis cracked his knuckles. "Is being hungry wrong? The Houston Rockets had a saying, 'Be humble. Be hungry.'"

Greatest irony of life: Our pursuit of temporary happiness steals our permanent happiness.

"That was decades ago! How do you know?"

"It's my Dad's favorite quote. He's repeated it a million times." Travis rolled his eyes.

Rishi laughed. "Love that saying. That's why the Rockets won back-to-back NBA championships. I remember, after they won, Suchi and I went to Richmond Street. Jam-packed with people and traffic, all nightclubs stayed open till the morning."

"Sounds like a blast," said Travis.

"Loads of fun! Incredible for Houston to win championships twice in a row! See, hungry in their case meant focus and commitment, not complacency," said Rishi.

"How does that square up with what you're saying?"

"When I say hungry," said Rishi, "I'm talking about the nature of the mind where it endlessly craves for more, gets bored with what you have, laments for what you've lost, fears to lose what you possess, and lives in constant anxiety about the future. As if that's not enough, the mind judges and compares you to others. So, even if your life is excellent, it'll depress itself thinking about how others have it better. That's crazy."

"And true," said Travis.

"The mind is obsessively, compulsively, possessive."

Travis smiled. "Is everyone's mind like that? I thought it was just me."

"Ask anyone, they'll admit their mind's restless and hungry." Rishi raised his index finger, "Now, it's possible they don't see it that way because they haven't thought about it."

> *The mind is obsessively, compulsively, possessive.*

Travis tapped his thumb on the sofa. "But, what's wrong with wanting more? Don't want to be bums, doing nothing."

"Not at all, we should be productive, otherwise society will decay. Work hard, make money, have a good family, and enjoy life. We should absolutely do that!"

"Did you just contradict yourself?" said Travis.

"No. There's no problem in enjoying life. The problem arises when the mind becomes solely dependent on external items for happiness. It doesn't know how to be happy by itself."

"That sounds weird. What do you mean?" said Travis.

"We can generate happiness internally," said Rishi. "But we're not tuned into that, our entire focus is external. Drug addicts aren't the only ones who are addicted, we all are." Rishi touched his forehead. "Our minds demand a higher and higher dose of things and emotions to feel the same high, otherwise, we become unhappy. This is a vicious cycle and robs us of our peace." In a soft tone, Rishi said, "And, we lose control when we lose something that's dear to us."

Rishi eyed Travis carefully to gauge if his remark had reminded Travis about Nathan. Travis did not react. Rishi felt comfortable and continued, "We're addicted to our careers, money, status, relationships, you name it. Ask anyone if he or she has too much money. No one will say yes."

Travis shook his head. "I'll never say that."

"Even a multi-billionaire won't," said Rishi.

"I don't see a problem with that," said Travis. "I don't believe the quote, 'Money is the root of all evil.'"

"Actually, the quote is, 'The love of money is the root of all evil,'" said Rishi. "It's the addiction to money that's bad."

Travis flared his nostrils.

Rishi lifted his palms halfway. "Fine, I'll give you other examples. An exercise buff, who loves the adrenalin rush, will push himself insanely and yet not once will you hear him say, 'I'm overdoing it,' even if he's harming his body."

"That's funny," said Travis. "I see them at the gym a lot. But, I know what you're saying. Some of them take steroids to build muscles, which is a baaaaad idea."

"Ask any woman if her husband could be a better spouse." Rishi smiled. "Every woman will say, 'Oh God, yes!'"

Travis put his left hand on his waist and pouted his lips. "Hey, have you been talking to my wife?"

"No, I've been talking to mine," replied Rishi.

Both laughed heartily.

"Your examples...," said Travis, "they're normal people. You really think we're addicts?"

"Absolutely. Since addiction happens over time, you feel it's normal. An addict doesn't recognize his addiction, he justifies it, I only smoke so many a day, I only drink so much, I only eat so much, I only play video games so much. I can give it up whenever I want. There's nothing wrong with alcohol, the question is does it have control over us or do we have control."

Travis nodded. "Do we know when enough is enough?"

"Take phones, teens to adults, we're all addicted," said Rishi. "Some people, if they wake up, check their phones even in the middle of the night. It's a full-blown addiction."

"I'm guilty of that," said Travis.

"Not a good habit," said Rishi. "Even successful movie stars share how they feel abject depression when their movies fail in a row. The need for constant success and adulation is a debilitating addiction."

"I don't like failure," said Travis. "I want every one of our apps to be a huge hit. I never saw it as an addiction."

"It's an addiction if failure sends you into a tailspin and causes deep depression. It's not just the desire for success, but the intense fear of failure can be an addiction too," said Rishi.

"Boy, you hit the nail on the head," said Travis. "Fear of failure is a big problem for me."

Rishi nodded. "Later, we'll discuss a few solutions for addressing anxiety. They've helped me." Rishi lifted two fingers. "Addictions are bad for two reasons. First, we become a slave to things. Second, and more important reason, addiction prevents spiritual growth. It prevents our mind from calming down. An acquaintance of mine started a business 20 years ago. Today, he makes $1 million a year."

Travis tapped the sofa's arm. "Good for him."

"To maximize profits he doesn't hire senior level people, so he has to work all the time," said Rishi.

"Makes no sense. He has the money, he should hire folks."

"When he started every penny mattered," said Rishi. "Saving every penny is so ingrained in his psyche, now it's a burden, it's become a prison."

"He's making good money, I don't see his problem," said Travis.

"You can have all the success and wealth," said Rishi, "but if your mind's addicted, you'll miss out on life. You —"

Enjoy the world, engage with it, just do not be addicted to it.

"Your examples," interrupted Travis with impatience in his voice, "are about the rich. Are the poor ready for spirituality?"

"No, no, this isn't about rich versus poor. Even a homeless person can be as possessive about his belongings."

"You're right," said Travis, "I've seen that."

"A middle-class family can worry constantly about their financial future and the future of their kids," said Rishi.

"I can relate to that, my parents worried a lot," said Travis.

Rishi turned dour. "Many people who face serious problems worry obsessively and lose the will to fight."

Travis closed his fist. "Everyone's gotta fight."

"Yes, but the fight's external and internal," said Rishi. "The internal fight's more critical. In bad situations, we lament what's gone wrong and imagine the worst outcomes. Our mind makes it worse by repeating it all the time, a horrible movie that plays non-stop. Our addiction is not just to the good things in life, we can get addicted to misery just as well."

Travis's face turned grim. He squeezed the sofa's arm.

Rishi glanced away. "I feel for the people who are trapped in their problems, suffocated by their own mind. Our mind can be the most potent source of our sadness and suffering. It can make our life a veritable hell on Earth. Addiction to misery is no fun."

> *Our mind can be the most potent source of our sadness and suffering.*

"I don't think anyone gets addicted to misery." Travis tapped his thumb. "Addiction's such an extreme word. Even your acquaintance, I won't say he's addicted, I'd say he's passionate about making money."

"There's a difference between passion and obsession," said Rishi. "Passion drives you, obsession possesses you. Passion lifts you, obsession drowns you."

"It's a narrow difference between the two," said Travis.

Rishi wagged his finger. "No, no, it's a big difference. Passion never causes you to lose perspective. Obsession leaves you with no perspective. When you're passionate, you listen well. If things don't go your way, you regroup and continue to apply yourself. When you obsess, you stop listening, you turn blind, you judge others, blame others, and find ways to silence those who disagree with you."

Passion lifts you, obsession drowns you.

"Okay, I see the difference. That's a great point, obsession versus passion," said Travis.

Rishi touched his wrist. "An obsessed mind can cause immense harm. People commit suicide or kill their lovers when their love is out of control. A dictator kills his own people when they rise against him because he's obsessed with his rule. Obsessions are our nemesis," said Rishi.

Travis shook his head. "Those are extreme cases. Normal people probably aren't as crazily obsessed."

"Okay, I'll share some common examples. Our political leaders are so obsessed with partisan politics they sacrifice the good of the country to serve their ideologies."

"Self-serving leeches," Travis pretended to dig his nails into his arm, "all they care about is themselves."

"At social gatherings," said Rishi, "rich men can't stop talking about how much money they're making, and the toys they're buying. They don't realize money's their obsession."

"Actually, showing off is their obsession." Travis rolled his eyes. "Even their kids can be so arrogant."

"Some couples are addicted to bickering," said Rishi. "They're obsessed with highlighting everything their spouse does wrong."

"A guy on my team constantly badmouths his wife," said Travis. "I never say anything bad about my wife, ever."

Rishi smiled. "Because you're afraid she'll find out."

Travis snapped his fingers. "Man, you know me too well."

"Take those who work all the time," said Rishi. "Working long hours to meet a deadline is okay, working long hours for decades robs people of their creativity and objectivity, makes them resistant to change. They never realize how work became a chronic obsession. They're workaholics."

Travis cringed remembering he is one but did not see anything wrong with it.

Rishi caressed his forehead. "All my life I've put extraordinary pressure on myself to succeed. No one has pressured me, not my parents, not my wife. But, something inside me wants to push hard. I'm very competitive. I'm my biggest critic, it drives me crazy... yet I can't stop."

Relish today! Do not let the past or the future stop you from enjoying today. Today will not come back.

Travis felt uneasy realizing he was not much different.

Rishi put his fist on his mouth. "I started with nothing...," Rishi took a deep breath, "in all these years, I can't remember one day when I didn't wake up worrying about my job, my career, my bonus, my promotion. I've never had to sleep hungry, and yet I've never stopped having tension about money."

"Money's the root of all tension for me too," said Travis.

Rishi's eyes drooped. "I'm as obsessed as my penny-pinching acquaintance. Twenty years have gone by, if only, instead of worrying obsessively I'd spent time relishing my life."

"I worry obsessively too," said Travis.

Like a father feeling for his son, Rishi said, "I know you do, and I'd love to stop you from making the mistakes I've made."

"Your personal example about worrying obsessively hit home for me," said Travis.

"Obsessions rob us of our peace," said Rishi. "I don't know if this is the case, but if you're obsessed with Travisto, you'll worry 24x7 about its future. Your objectivity will suffer and you'll ignore warning signs

> *Managed fire is very useful, unmanaged fire can cause great harm. Manage your mind.*

to change course. Your obsession could become your undoing."

Travis tensed up, his mind full of crosscurrents, feelings to admit things were bad and conflicting feelings to defend his company. Travis retreated into the sofa.

"May I share a story about obsession," asked Rishi.

"I love stories," said Travis.

"In ancient times," said Rishi, "there was a rich kingdom that would randomly select an ordinary person to be king every five years. That person would rule the country and enjoy all the lavish luxuries. It was the biggest jackpot in the land. The only condition was at the end of the five years a boatman would transport the king to an island with wild animals. Which meant the king would be eaten alive."

"I wouldn't want to be king there," said Travis.

Rishi smiled. "One year they selected a wise man to be king. When his time was over, he came down from the palace happy and said his goodbyes with great joy."

"Okay," said Travis.

"When the boatman was transporting the king, he asked, 'Sir, are you okay?' The king replied, 'I'm fine. Why do you ask?' The boatman said, 'In thirty years, I've transported many previous kings. All of them came down from the palace crying. By the time I'd reach halfway to the island they'd panic and want to jump off the boat. Do you know what awaits you?'"

"What did the king say?" asked Travis.

"The king said, 'Oh, my good boatman, our people have fantasized so much about the king's luxuries, enjoying those luxuries has become an obsession among everyone. On their selection, the previous kings couldn't believe their luck and were sucked into spending all their time enjoying the good life. They forgot their time would come to an end."

"I see where the story is headed," said Travis.

"Wait, here's the main part," said Rishi, "The King continued, 'I enjoyed the luxuries but I never forgot what the future held for me. I've built a palace on the island, killed all the wild animals, and my family is waiting there for me.'"

Travis's eyes widened. "Wow. I didn't see that coming. I thought you were going to make a point about fixing obsession, but preparing for the next stage... that's beautiful."

"When we become obsessed we miss the big picture," said Rishi. "You know this, we have boom and bust cycles in the economy and in the stock market. I remember at the height of the last boom, so many technology companies went through an IPO to raise money in the stock market. Many of the CEOs became billionaires overnight, at least on paper."

"And, they lost it all when the market crashed," said Travis.

"Yes," said Rishi, "in boom times, those CEOs and their investors forgot the boom can end without

> *When we become obsessed we miss the big picture.*

warning. Their mind became hungry for more and once the obsession had taken hold they couldn't see the fire until it was too close."

"I've read those stories," said Travis. "I really liked the king-boatman story. We must be careful not to be obsessed."

Rishi smiled in satisfaction. "Very nice." He touched his forehead. "I want to talk about the most potent form of our obsession. It envelopes us and we don't even realize it."

Travis raised his eyebrows. "Wow, okay."

> *Have passion, but no obsessions. Our obsessions and addictions keep us from becoming happy and peaceful.*

> *Our own mind can be the biggest source of our unhappiness, anxiety and stress in life.*

Chapter 4: Mind's Bubble

"The mind's capable of an incredible phenomenon," said Rishi, "it can project its own bubble,"

"Bubble?" asked Travis.

"Yes, the mind can create its own world," said Rishi. "It creates, or I should say, projects your identity and your ego. We're enslaved by the image of ourselves our mind creates. We assign our own self-importance and operate on that basis. Then we expect and demand a certain level of lifestyle, respect, adulation, love, success, or whatever else floats our boat."

"Our mind gets obsessed to its bubble. Is this our trap?" asked Travis.

"It's the most dangerous form of obsession," said Rishi. "The addiction to our own ego."

"I never thought of that," said Travis.

The addiction to our ego is the most dangerous form of obsession.

"Have you watched professional athletes and coaches?" said Rishi, "Some of them are so self-absorbed, they can't evaluate themselves objectively."

"With you brother, they're self-obsessed. Watching their press conferences, I've wanted to grab and shake them."

"Easy now," said Rishi smiling. "Obsession with our self-importance creates an overinflated ego which can lead to a train-wreck. A doctor who's full of himself will refuse to accept his patient could be served better with an alternate treatment."

Travis made no comment.

"Take CEOs," said Rishi, "many think there's no one else as smart as them."

"Wait a minute, they are super smart," defended Travis, in awe of the Silicon Valley CEOs.

"No doubt, CEOs are smart people," said Rishi. "The problem is when their mind clouds their judgment and they become insular. Their ego can become a big problem."

Travis tapped his thumb. "Have the best one, MBAs are so brainwashed by their schools. They think they're the greatest thing since sliced bread."

"Schools teach students business skills but not life skills," said Rishi. "But the rest of us aren't much better. We're drinking our own Kool-Aid, caught up in our bubbles.

> *Schools teach students business skills but not life skills.*

Every executive in my team thinks they're always right and the others are wrong. I, of course, think I'm always right." Rishi laughed. "We're so caught up in our own thinking."

Travis nodded, a little pensive. He prided on being right.

"Let me drive the point about being caught up in our bubble," said Rishi. "We're like a well-frog."

"A what?"

"A frog who's born in a well, grows there to become an adult, and dies there," said Rishi.

"Okay," said Travis.

"The frog thinks his well is the entire world. He never realizes there's an ocean out there beyond his wildest imagination."

"First, I thought the well would be such a confining space," said Travis. "But all the frog knows is the well. He's happy there. He doesn't know any better."

"Like the well-frog, we're caught in our life's bubble. Instead of seeing infinite spirituality, we see the world from our limited, narrow and materialistic perspective, plus we're convinced ours is the only valid perspective."

"With you, man, with you," said Travis.

"I want to share a story about mind bubbles," said Rishi. "This story always tugs at me."

"Okay," said Travis a bit excited.

"One day, while riding through the marketplace, a king saw an old lady selling dried fish. He invited her to the palace to let her enjoy it for a day. He liked hearing from his courtiers what a good king he was."

"Okay." Travis had an amused look.

"At the palace, they served the old lady all the nicest food dishes at dinner, entertained her, and at the end of the day retired her to one of the palace rooms. It had a large soft bed, gold lined headboard, fine linen coverings, and rose petals in water pots all over the room and other aromatic scents."

"Sounds wonderful."

"Yes. The next morning the King invited the woman to his court. He expected her to come in and say she loved the rich experience, and she was grateful for his generosity."

"Then?" said Travis.

"The lady arrived. The king asked in front of his courtiers, 'Did you enjoy? Did you have a wonderful night?' She replied, 'I didn't sleep one wink. Was the worst night of my life!'"

"Really?" said Travis.

"Yes. Upset and embarrassed, the king asked, 'Why, was the bed not comfortable? I'll execute the person who was supposed to take care of you.'"

"Man! What did the woman say?" said Travis.

"She replied, 'The bed was fine, the room was great, but I couldn't sleep because I missed my basket of fish. I'm used to the smell of fish, I can't sleep without it.' Taken aback, the king looked down at the lady, and asked sarcastically, 'You're used to the smell of rotten fish, hence you couldn't sleep?' She replied, 'Yes, your majesty.' The king dismissed her."

"That's interesting," said Travis.

Rishi unfurled his fingers. "When he overcame his anger and embarrassment the king realized fish is the old lady's life. That's what she wants and that's all she cares for."

"That's her bubble, that's her well," said Travis.

"It became an eye-opening spiritual lesson for the king."

"How?" asked Travis.

"The old lady had such a wonderful opportunity to enjoy the palace's pleasures, but she couldn't because she was caught up in her own bubble. The king realized he's no different from the old lady. He wondered what he was missing out in life because he was caught up in his bubble. He leaves his palace and the kingdom in search of the true meaning of life."

We are all caught up in our mind-bubbles.

Rishi paused and closed his eyes. He slowed down his breathing. Travis reflected on the story. "That's powerful!" Travis wiggled. "Gave me a shiver."

"How so?" asked Rishi.

"You've been saying we're obsessed with our bubble, but it didn't sink in until I heard the story," said Travis. "Both the woman and the king are trapped in their wells. One is a stinky well and the other is a palatial well, but they're both wells." Travis brushed his hair aside. "I'm caught up in my well too."

"We all are," said Rishi as he took a deep breath, "and, all the while the ocean of spirituality waits patiently for us. Like the king-boatman story, we're living our lives caught in our obsessions oblivious that our time's limited. We must overcome our obsessions and make the preparations now to travel to the ocean of spirituality."

Travis leaned forward. "Wow! All right, okay, how do we leave our well? How do we reduce our obsessions?"

"By managing our mind!" said Rishi. "The techniques for managing our mind will help us reduce our anxiety and stress, and, most importantly, help us find peace."

"What are these techniques?" asked Travis.

"I will share them with you. It's a detailed discussion because these are not gimmicky techniques, they're serious but simple techniques. They have the power to transform our lives. The question we must ask ourselves — can we leave our well to experience the ocean? Can we step back from our obsessions to attain the ultimate?"

"What is the ultimate?" asked Travis.

"We're going to discuss spirituality next. I'll answer then what is the ultimate? It's the most important aspect of our life."

*Recognize you are living
in your mind's bubble, in your mind's
limited egocentric well.*

*Pierce your mind's bubble,
leave the limited well to experience the
infinite ocean of spirituality!*

Chapter 5: Happy Soul

Rishi caressed his forehead. "In the last few years, especially the last two, my thoughts about spirituality have crystallized more and I see the pieces of the puzzle coming together."

"Cool," said Travis.

"Yeah, but I'm still testing to see if I'm right." Rishi slightly raised his palm. "I should say that differently, I'm still figuring out what I'm missing. You see, I haven't really discussed this with anyone. So you're my… well, my guinea pig. Is that okay?"

Travis tapped his thumb. "That's fine."

"Now, be gentle if you don't like something I share."

Travis smiled. "I'll be nice."

Rishi held his hand up in the air. "Let's talk spirituality from a thirty thousand feet level. I want to start with the basics and build from there. It'll help me stay coherent."

"That'd be good," said Travis. "I could use a refresher."

Rishi pressed his palms against his chest and lowered his head slightly. "Spirituality is about connecting with our spirit, our soul." He gently caressed his right fist with his left palm. "Our soul is the consciousness in us that gives us significance."

Travis nodded.

"This soul is our life-force," Rishi stretched his arms apart, "it makes the whole world come alive for us. Without consciousness we can't perceive the world, we can't interact with the world. When the soul departs, the body dies and loses its dynamism. This spiritual energy keeps our bodies functioning, without it our body is just matter."

"You're calling the life in us as the soul?" said Travis.

"Yes, life, soul, spirit, are all synonyms," replied Rishi.

"Does it exist? Does the soul really exist?" asked Travis.

"Modern-day scientists haven't pinpointed where the soul resides in the body, they haven't been able to demonstrate energy leaving the body at the time of death. So, I'll —"

Travis interjected, "Didn't mean to challenge you on that."

"It's a valid question," said Rishi. "I haven't seen scientific evidence for the existence of the soul, that said, I go on three aspects. First, all the religions talk about the soul. Second, the ancient sages talk about experiencing energy as it travels through the spine and brain, invigorating the seven major energy centers in the body. Third, I do know as a scientific fact, whenever this energy leaves, the body goes limp. This life-force keeps all living things living."

"That says it all." Travis gave a firm nod. "Some people say the soul is in our heart."

"I... don't think that's true," said Rishi. "People who have a heart transplant do not get a new soul. The soul is probably the energy in the spinal cord and the brain, but I don't have a proof for it."

Travis shrugged. "That's okay."

Rishi touched together the fingers of both hands. "Albert Einstein has said energy can't be created or destroyed, it can only be transformed. He's describing Physics, but it's one of the most profound spiritual statements. The spiritual energy in you and me can never be destroyed."

Travis slowly moved his head back and forth, going over the statements. "Special energy keeps us alive. Energy can't be destroyed. The soul is —"

"Permanent. The soul is permanent!" declared Rishi.

Travis narrowed his eyebrows, amused by the declaration. "I can't argue with that." He had a faint smile. "Might change form, but it's got to be permanent."

"Bingo," said Rishi with excitement. "The soul, our soul, our spiritual energy is permanent, it might change, but it can't be destroyed."

Travis had a straight look on his face.

Rishi became a little self-conscious. "I haven't pulled wool over your eyes, it's logic."

"No, I get it." Travis shifted on the sofa. "Not questioning it, in fact, I'm tickled, it's that straightforward."

Rishi smiled. "Isn't that amazing, and it doesn't require a leap of faith. Science and spirituality aren't at odds. They're both about the truths in this world. If we search for truth, our lives will be heavenly."

Travis nodded. "Cool."

Rishi looked endearingly at Travis. "Spirituality has the power to change our lives. It's as if we have this infinite ocean of bliss… this ocean of peace inside of us. All we have to do is immerse in this ocean." Rishi gently rubbed his feet on the silk rug.

> *We have an infinite ocean of bliss inside of us. We must immerse in this ocean.*

"Don't be like the well-frog," said Travis. "Leave the mind's limited well and immerse in the ocean of spirituality."

"Yes, dissolve in this ocean, become one with it. The spiritual energy in us, our soul is the center of infinite bliss and happiness. Our soul is happy. Actually, happy may not be the best word. I don't have the right word —"

"Why?" said Travis.

"Happy means you can be unhappy too. Happy and sad are counterparts. The soul is never unhappy, emotions don't affect it. The soul is pure bliss! Pure peace! All the time! Always! It doesn't waver. It's pure blissful energy," said Rishi.

Our true inherent nature is pure peace.

"Soul is above emotions, that's why it's happy?" said Travis.

"Umm... I want to restate or clarify what I said. It's not that the soul is happy or blissful. The soul is emotionless, it's stateless. It's our experience of the soul that makes us infinitely happy and blissful. It's the happiness derived from connecting with the soul. There, I like that better."

"Is that a leap of faith or do you have proof?" asked Travis.

"I was anticipating that question," said Rishi.

"You said challenge."

"I did, I did, and it's good," said Rishi. "For now, let me just say the experience of the soul is happy and blissful. And, I say that based on personal experience. I've experienced glimmers of the soul, of that peace. I don't have to rely on someone else's writings or teachings, this is a self-experience."

To tease Rishi, Travis gave him a skeptical look.

"No, no, I'm not being slippery," said Rishi. "This is more about showing than talking. I can tell you the soul experience is happy, but you need to experience it. Only when you taste it, you'll know for sure. That'd be the most definitive proof."

Travis's face brightened. "That's what I tell our investors too. Don't trust us, try our apps then you'll know for sure."

Rishi felt good with Travis's engagement and said, "Spirituality is the Universe's most amazing gift to humans." Rishi had a look on his face you would find on the face of a teenager in love for the first time. "Our spiritual ability allows us to connect with the soul. The day we start establishing contact with the soul in us, our lives change forever. We begin to experience infinite bliss and happiness. We become truly blessed. While on Earth physically, we start experiencing a heavenly state."

Rishi closed his eyes for a moment. Then he said, "Your soul is the divine. There is nothing more divine in this Universe than your soul. It is divinity in our presence and in ourselves."

Travis sat up straight. "Wow!"

"Experiencing your soul is the best thing you can do with your life. It'll give you peace and calm, like nothing else, and it'll stay with you. Every other pleasure and happiness fades away with time, it's tentative and unreliable. Connecting with your soul is the most fulfilling, most transformative aspect of your life."

Rishi raised his index finger. "If we're not making spiritual progress we're wasting our lives."

"That's why I'm here," said Travis.

"I know. And, I'm going to do my best to share what I know so you can progress on this journey. I hope I can help you transform your life, that is the goal… I know that sounds bold."

"Not at all, I'm counting on you, buddy," said Travis. "I need a transformation." Travis's phone vibrated. He paused deciding whether he should answer it. He wanted to answer it but decided not to. He looked back at Rishi.

"Next, I'll share with you a statement which to me is the simplest and the grandest statement regarding our spiritual journey," said Rishi. "It's really simple and incredibly powerful at the same time. I'm really excited to share it."

"Cool," said Travis. "I'm all ears."

"But let me enjoy the peace in this moment for a second...." Rishi closed his eyes and lifted his head, peace reflecting on his face.

Spirituality is the Universe's most amazing gift for you!

Chapter 6: Spiritual Muntruh

Travis watched Rishi's peaceful face. Rishi opened his eyes and looked at Travis as a mother lovingly looks at her child.

Travis smiled. "So, how do we become spiritual?"

"With practice and discipline. It can be a long path."

Travis narrowed his eyebrows. "Why?"

Rishi grimaced. "One major stumbling block."

"Our deeds?"

"No." Rishi touched his forehead. "Our mind! It prevents us from experiencing this most beautiful ocean of bliss within us. We can be so stupid, missing out on the deepest happiness of our lives and not even realize it!"

"Because of our obsessions and addictions?"

"Yes, our hungry mind is the reason why we struggle unnecessarily in our lives." Rishi raised his index finger. "We need the mind to survive in the material world —"

"Material world?" asked Travis.

"The physical, sensory and emotional world we live in," said Rishi. "We perceive the material world through our five senses of sight, hearing, smell, taste, and touch. Our mind experiences the world colored by our emotions, feelings, and expectations. The material world's essentially everything external to us."

"And, the spiritual world is internal to us?" asked Travis.

"Yes, the spiritual world is internal to us, untainted, unaffected by the material world," said Rishi. "Our problem is when our mind is engrossed, all we perceive and feel is the material world. It overpowers us and doesn't let us experience the internal spiritual world."

"Why? How?" said Travis with an unsure look.

Rishi looked away for a brief second. "When the water in the pond is choppy, your reflection is distorted and difficult to see. When the water is still, you can see your reflection clearly."

"So the mind has to be still?" asked Travis.

"Yes, when the mind is quiet —"

"Like when it's sleeping?" said Travis.

"No, when you're in deep sleep your mind is absent, that does you no good. Your mind has to be present but must be completely still. When the mind is calm with no thoughts, then can the soul shine through and you can experience it."

Travis was lost. He tapped his fingers on the sofa's arm.

Rishi spanned the room as he moistened his lips. "Ah, let me try another example." He looked at Travis. "Your mind is the bouncer outside the nightclub who won't allow you to go in to meet your soul. The soul is the pop star inside the nightclub. If you don't meet the star, your trip's a waste."

Travis's eyes lit up. "Never heard you describe it like that."

"Just thought about it." Rishi took a bow. "If you don't get to make it inside, you'll never know how wonderful that experience is, even though you've spent hours waiting outside."

"Makes sense, so how can I ask the bouncer to let me in?"

"That's the most important question of your life." Rishi's energy rose. "Nothing in your life will have a bigger impact than figuring that out."

"Ooh!" Travis wiggled his body in jest.

"No kidding." Rishi smiled with encouragement. "Most of us live our lives never making it inside the nightclub. We miss out on the Universe's most beautiful gift to human beings."

Travis digested Rishi's logic.

"Who's a famous pop star these days?" asked Rishi.

If we do not experience our souls, we will miss out on the most valuable thing in our lives.

"Lady Gaga, Katy Perry, Drake, Justin Bieber...."

"Imagine a Justin Bieber concert," said Rishi. "Imagine if you're a teenage girl who's invited backstage to have her hand kissed by Justin. Imagine the absolute bliss you'd experience."

Travis smiled mischievously. "Bieber is our life's goal?"

Rishi feigned a dirty look. "Meeting our soul is the most exhilarating experience we can ever have. A Bieber fan —"

"You mean a Belieber?" Travis smiled.

Rishi rolled his eyes in jest. "Fine, a Belieber can be in a daze after meeting her idol. She could forget all aspects of her life, including her loving boyfriend. Spirituality is so powerful it can color your entire life, and unlike the Bieber encounter, once you've experienced the ultimate happiness, it never wears off."

Fascinated by the discussion, Travis listened carefully. "Belieber for life," said Travis and before Rishi could give him another dirty look he quickly added, "Ok, I'll drop it."

Rishi pressed his thumb and finger. "We aren't making enough spiritual progress. I know I'm not. It should be our number one priority."

"Can't drop everything else. Should we?" asked Travis.

"No, no, fulfill your duties, but the material world is the side act," said Rishi. "Spirituality is the real reason we're here. You need to remind yourself that standing in the line outside the club, even though it may be fun, doesn't come close to what lies inside. The material world is truly pleasurable, but spirituality is at another level, there's no comparison."

"It's like building apps is fun, but the real fun is in making a boatload of money. That's exciting," said Travis. "So, focus on the important thing, focus on spirituality."

"Yes! Every day! If we don't experience our souls, we'll miss out on the most valuable thing in our life."

"In your example, only a few meet the star."

"Darn," Rishi snapped his fingers, "I should've thought of a better analogy. Remember who's the bouncer?"

The material world is just the side act. Spirituality is the real reason we are here.

"Our mind."

"That's right, the bouncer is your own mind. You're not competing with anyone else, you're fighting with your own mind. And, you're not fighting to meet someone else's soul, this is a fight to meet your own soul. Everyone's pop star, their heartthrob is their own soul."

"You know, I've read some people describe this world as a simulation or even a video game," said Travis.

"I've read that too. And, let me make this addition to that analogy," said Rishi. "We're all playing at a certain level in the video game of life. We are opening rooms and chests, finding ammunition and treasures, trying to be the best. But even if we come first, we are still stuck at that same level."

"So, figure out how to go the next level," said Travis.

"Yes, we can collect all the wealth, reputation, relationships in the material world, but we'll still be stuck here. We must figure out how to get to the next level — the spiritual level."

Travis snapped his fingers. "Have to win the game of life."

"Yeah, we do!" Rishi beamed. "I had promised to share with you this really simple, yet incredibly powerful statement regarding our spiritual journey. It's a muntruh."

"A what?" said Travis.

"People say mantra, but the original Sanskrit pronunciation is muntruh. Mun pronounced like run, truh like truffle."

"Got it, mun-truh," said Travis.

"Good. Mun stands for mind, and truh means instrument. Muntruh is an instrument for the mind. It influences how your mind thinks, and channels your thoughts and feelings."

"Okay," said Travis.

"The muntruh I'm about to share with you is the most profound statement I can share with you about our spiritual pursuit." Rishi opened his palm wide and then closed it tight. "It's the essence, the synopsis of everything I can ever discuss."

"Okay." Travis sat up, his attention fully focused on Rishi.

In an emphatic tone, Rishi recited, "Quiet your hungry mind, let your happy soul shine."

Rishi took a deep breath. Moving his hands like an orchestra conductor, he repeated it with a change, "Quiet my hungry mind, let my happy soul shine." Rishi reabsorbed every word as he said it aloud. "Can you say it?"

Travis obliged. "Quiet my hungry mind, let my happy soul shine."

Rishi paused for the sentence to register. "All you've to do in your spiritual quest — is to quiet your mind. Once your mind calms down, your soul will naturally and automatically shine through in you in its full glory, delivering infinite happiness!"

Rishi punched his fist in the air. "That's it. That is it! That is the ultimate spiritual pursuit statement! It can't get any simpler, it can't get any grander."

Rishi stood up in excitement, his honey colored eyes glistening as if they were shining diamonds. At 6 feet 2 inches, he was taller than the average Indian height. His slightly muscular built made him look bigger than his medium sized frame.

Quiet Your Hungry Mind, Let Your Happy Soul Shine!

Travis looked up at Rishi mesmerized by the intense look on his face. Rishi looked towering, resplendent in the significance of what he had said.

Taken aback, Travis's mind feverishly processed what he had just heard. He looked away and then back at Rishi who was still standing radiantly. Travis felt intimated. Rishi relaxed and sat down, still beaming.

"Is that it?" Travis contorted his torso. "Is that really it?"

"Yes, absolutely!" said Rishi in a soft, professorial tone, not displaying the excitement that had just a minute ago sprung him to his feet. "There are hundreds of thousands of pages of religious scriptures about the pursuit of spirituality, plus the millions of pages of interpretations by people who've come after the great ancient sages, messiahs, and prophets."

Rishi moved his hands to gesture a large sphere. "If you boil down the entire ocean of spiritual scriptures, it all comes down to this muntruh." He took a deep breath, held his right forefinger up and in a deep voice reiterated, "Quiet your hungry mind, let your happy soul shine."

Rishi interlocked his fingers and closed his eyes to let his own words sink into him. His face turned peaceful. Travis watched in wonderment and skepticism mixed. Rishi opened his eyes.

"Can it be... that simple?" questioned Travis. His face looked guilty as if he was stealing cookies from the cookie jar.

Rishi took a few breaths. "It is! Simple but very difficult. Calming our mind — where it is completely quiet — is the most difficult challenge of our life. And, that my friend is the game of life. The day you quiet your mind, will be the first day of your true journey, until then you're just thrashing around, wasting your time waiting outside the nightclub."

"Is that the day I'll meet my soul?" asked Travis.

"Not yet," said Rishi, amused a little, "that's the day the bouncer steps aside and lets you enter your inner chambers. It'll take some time for your soul's brilliance to shine through, but you'll be on the path."

Travis stood up. He pushed the hair off his forehead and looked at Rishi seated on the sofa. Immersed in his statement, Rishi had a gentle smile adorning his face.

Stepping away from the sitting area, Travis slowly paced along the windows. His steps landing gently on the hardwood floor, he walked back and forth for a few minutes and then looked at Rishi. "You've talked about spirituality before, but never tied it down to a single statement."

"Power lies in simplicity, not in complexity. Some of the most powerful axioms in life are very simple," said Rishi.

"I'm trying to understand... I mean... you know... what you said isn't complex, it's simple... I'm just —"

"Struggling to accept it?"

Travis squirmed and twisted. "Yup... can't believe —"

"You can't believe I boiled all of it down," said Rishi.

"Sort of... like you tied a nice bow... and now here it is," said Travis directly without hesitation or consideration for Rishi's feelings. "I've thought about spirituality even after I left Houston. Read about it and watched stuff... but didn't —"

Rishi interjected, "And your struggle is?"

"...Figured we'd have a longer discussion," said Travis.

Rishi sighed and looked down. "If I'd shared the statement after I'd built it up for hours, dressed it up, then you'd go yeah makes sense. If I give it to you plainly, you don't respect it." Rishi shook his head. "Now, I'm questioning myself if I should be sharing all of this... I don't know if you'll value it."

Travis twisted uncomfortably. "I... I need to appreciate it more. I see you value it, I wanna see what you're seeing."

"Okay," said Rishi, "come have a seat, don't be afraid."

"Me afraid? Nah!" Travis did a Karate pose with his hands and walked back to take his seat smiling. Rishi smiled too.

"It's taken me years to realize this statement is it," said Rishi. "I've wondered how this muntruh can be so simple, but as I've contemplated, I see how powerful it is. Everything I know points to this. Every time I learn something, I test to see if the muntruh holds — and it does every time. I've not seen another statement as succinct as this." Rishi ran his hand over his forehead. "I'm rambling."

"You're fine. I'm with you," said Travis.

"Let's test if it's the truth, and if it is then we should accept it and if not then we don't," said Rishi. "Is that acceptable?"

Travis felt better. "I'm ready to understand your muntruh." Travis spoke in a tone a husband uses when he wants to make peace with his wife. "I'm sure you have a lot of meaning in it."

Just as a teacher who has immeasurable patience, Rishi felt he should do his best to help Travis understand the muntruh. He took his rimless glasses off and put them on the side table. He put his fist to his mouth, and closed his eyes, deep in thought.

Travis relaxed his body but was still a little antsy. Rishi's large forehead reflected some of the light coming from the windows.

Rishi opened his eyes. Travis gave him a faint smile. Rishi said, "I went through the items we need to discuss in detail, so you can appreciate this muntruh and see why it's so profound."

"Okay," said Travis without much enthusiasm.

"I was going to discuss spirituality in detail and then discuss managing our mind." Rishi sighed. "That's a logical order, but, I'll change the order so —"

"No, no," interrupted Travis, "please don't change the order. Do it the way you intended."

Rishi looked unsure.

"Please, listen, I'm sorry," said Travis. "My reaction was too strong. I need to listen first before I jump to judgment."

"That's quite all right," said Rishi, "Maybe I'm not handling pushbacks as well as I used to. That said, I'm perfectly okay with you pushing back, your pushbacks are very helpful."

"I know, but I need to have a little more patience," said Travis. "So, please continue in the order you were thinking and I'm sure it'll all make sense in the end."

"It will," said Rishi. "Let's do this. Let me give you a glimpse under the hood, show you the spiritual path, and then let's discuss managing our mind. I promise you, you'll see how this statement is the key to accessing our spiritual treasure. You'll appreciate it for its... mind-boggling-ness!"

Travis nodded ready to test Rishi's statement.

Quiet My Hungry Mind,

Let My Happy Soul Shine!

This statement is the KEY

to accessing our spiritual treasure!

Understand it. Implement it.

Chapter 7: Spiritual Path

Rishi walked over to a desk near the bookshelves behind the staircase. He pulled out a writing pad. He sat back down on the sofa, drew a diagram and showed it to Travis.

Spiritual Path

*"Quiet your hungry mind,
let your happy soul shine!"*

● Be regular & persistent

Quiet your Mind

● Have zero expectations

Quiet your Mind

Your Soul will unveil more

Mature your Perspectives

Finally Infinite Happiness will arise in you!

Your Soul will unveil bit by bit

Mature your Perspectives

Transform your Thoughts

Transform your Thoughts

© Ravi Kathuria

Travis smiled. "I've never seen a diagram for spirituality."

Rishi smiled. "You know I make presentations for a living."

"Welcome to the modern-era of spirituality," said Travis as he grinned.

"That's right," said Rishi as he did a thumbs up. "I want to explain spirituality in a modern way, where it's not buried in complexity and shrouded in mystery. I want to open it up, I want to shed light, let people realize it's simple, straightforward and achievable." Rishi thrust his chest forward. "That's the contribution I want to make to the world."

"Great speech, you win the first prize." Travis chuckled. Before Rishi could give him a dirty look, Travis said, "Just kidding."

"I know," said Rishi as he smiled.

"I like that actually," said Travis as he looked closely at the diagram. "I think this diagram will make it easier for me. Otherwise, it just becomes a lot of talk."

"I agree. This diagram helps me crystallize and categorize all the points I have in my mind," said Rishi. "Let me explain it." As a caring teacher, Rishi looked at Travis and in a comforting tone said, "When we expand the muntruh we arrive at the spiritual path. As you can see, the spiritual path is a spiral." Rishi gestured a spiral with his index finger.

Travis nodded watching Rishi's hand movements.

"A spiral in which you progress from one cycle to the next inner cycle, until you reach the center," said Rishi.

"Got it," said Travis.

"Each cycle has three parts you must work on, and one part that happens automatically, nature does it for you."

"Automatically?" said Travis.

"Yes. That's the amazing part about spirituality. You do the three parts and the rest is taken care of. First, transform your thoughts, second, mature your perspectives, and third, quiet your mind. When you execute these three steps, your soul will automatically unveil itself bit by bit."

Travis lifted three fingers in sequence, as he said, "Transform thoughts, mature perspectives, quiet the mind." He opened his palm. "Soul will unveil."

"Yes, but remember these steps are part of one cycle," said Rishi. "In the next cycle —"

"They repeat," said Travis gesturing a circle with his finger.

"Yes. In each successive cycle, you'll transform your thoughts more, mature your perspectives more, quiet your mind further, and your soul will become more and more evident. The steps don't have to be sequential. They can and do happen concurrently."

"Spiral ends when?" asked Travis tapping his thumb gently.

"When your mind is completely quiet and your soul shines in its fullest glory," said Rishi.

"That's realization?" asked Travis.

"That is self-realization, nirvana, whatever else you want to call it. You experience your soul fully, your true essence."

"That's when you experience infinite happiness?"

"Yes!" Rishi smiled. "That's when you meet your pop star. The most valuable jackpot of your life. Life will never be the same again. You'll be filled with unending bliss."

"Wow!" said Travis.

"That's the spiritual path!" Rishi clapped his hands displaying the excitement of a student at the science fair after her experiment delivers the desired result.

Travis basked in Rishi's excitement and positive energy. He felt his being uplifted.

"Once you experience total bliss," said Rishi, "you view the world, your own body and mind for what it is."

"What do you mean?"

"Once you experience the soul, your worldly identifications, desires, addictions and obsessions, your identity and ego, all melt away. When you —"

Rishi stopped mid-sentence and closed his eyes. He gently placed his left palm on his right wrist and folded his legs on the sofa. Breathing very slowly, Rishi's eye movements slowed.

> *Once you experience your soul, your worldly identifications, your addictions, your own identity and ego, all fade away.*

Travis watched Rishi become completely still. He watched in admiration. He wanted to fold his legs but realized he had his shoes on. He closed his eyes too and relaxed back in his seat.

After a few minutes, Rishi opened his eyes and reached for his glass of water. Travis heard him and opened his eyes too.

"Did you experience peace?" asked Travis in a soft voice.

Rishi nodded still a little adrift. He brought his focus back to the conversation. "Spirituality's truly amazing! What a gift!"

"Did you experience nirvana?"

Rishi smiled. "No, I didn't experience nirvana. I'm a long ways away. I've to work on it."

"You seemed so peaceful?"

"Yeah, sure, but this is just a marker on the way. The soul reveals itself bit by bit. Every time you experience true internal peace, you're experiencing a little bit of your soul."

"But it's not the ultimate?" asked Travis.

"Not yet. To reach the ultimate experience I've to quiet my mind a lot more and regularly experience these moments of bliss. Then one day, I'll experience the ultimate." Rishi tilted his head slightly, a peaceful look on his face.

"Very cool!" said Travis.

"Pretty cool." Rishi smiled, exhaling slowly. He took a few breaths, a beautiful smile on his face. "When you experience your soul, the material world and your own ego lose their stronghold on you. You become free and permanently happy."

"Completely happy?"

"Yes, absolutely, I guarantee it!" Rishi touched his chest.

Travis tilted. "I'll hunt you down if it doesn't happen."

Rishi smiled. "You know where I live."

"I do." Travis smiled too.

"People often say, I'm looking for a soul mate," said Rishi.

"Sure," said Travis.

"But the real thing is —" said Rishi.

"What?" interjected Travis.

"Patience, my friend…," Rishi blinked, "the best mate of all is your own soul. Your soul is your true mate. Once you experience your soul, you don't need any other mate."

"My soul completes me," said Travis distorting a famous line from a Hollywood movie. He grinned and pressed his palms against his chest

"Mr. Cheesyhead!" Rishi smiled.

"What you experience, is it really the soul?" asked Travis.

"Very intelligent question," said Rishi.

Travis nodded slightly.

"When you're completely peaceful, you don't feel your senses such as hearing or touch, you don't feel your body or your limbs, and your mind is completely quiet. Sometimes you experience energy vibrations up and down your spine and brain. I believe that is our life-force, our soul," said Rishi. "When you're peaceful, the only thing you do experience is the quiet presence of your own awareness or consciousness. Sometimes you even drift past that."

"Then what happens?" asked Travis.

"You experience the infinite, beyond the dimensions of time and space. You lose awareness of your own awareness."

Travis looked intrigued.

Rishi continued, "Your awareness or consciousness silences itself leaving you with a feeling of nothingness. At that point, you experience the soul, your divine energy. You become one with your soul. When the mind is quiet, when awareness itself is silent, incredible internal happiness begins to fill your being. That experience of your divine energy, giving you complete happiness, is self-realization!"

Rishi raised his finger. "Achieving infinite happiness is the highest purpose of our lives. Nothing else is as important."

"Nothing else matters?"

> *The Highest Purpose of our lives is to quiet our hungry minds, so we can feel our souls and experience infinite happiness.*

"It sort of matters because you've got to live and act in this world. You've got to do it, but the real purpose and payoff of human life is to achieve infinite and permanent happiness!"

Travis nodded.

Rishi continued, "Health, wealth, career, fame, artistic and scientific pursuits, family, love, faith, community, and religious service, are honorable and necessary pursuits, but they are needs and wants of our mind, not the ultimate purpose of our life. Focus on the ultimate!"

Travis raised his hand.

"My ultimate purpose!"

"Yes," said Rishi.

"Your ultimate purpose and your destiny! Every person on Earth, his or her destiny is this pure happiness. Sadly, people are not aware of it and aren't making progress towards achieving it."

"How do I achieve it?" asked Travis.

"Remember the three steps of the spiritual path? When we discuss managing our mind, we'll discuss them in detail, for now, let me go over them at a high level."

> *Health, wealth, career, fame, artistic and scientific pursuits, family, love, faith, community and religious service, are honorable and necessary pursuits, but they are needs and wants of our mind, not "The Ultimate Purpose of Our life."*

"Okay," said Travis.

"The first step is to transform your thoughts," said Rishi.

"How?" asked Travis.

"We engage with the world in the wrong manner, it causes anxiety and stress," said Rishi. "If we transform our thoughts, our stress will melt away. That's a powerful discussion I can't wait to have with you."

"Boy, do I need my stress to melt away," said Travis.

"It will. The second step is to mature your perspectives on life perseveringly," said Rishi.

"Perseveringly, you love these two-dollar words, don't you, Mr. Ph.D.!" Travis grinned.

"Excuse me!" Rishi rocked his head back and forth sideways in the typical Indian fashion to play along. "First of all my Ph.D. is in Computer Science, not in English. Second, perseveringly isn't a two dollar word, it's only a ten cent word."

"Buddy, I was almost a college dropout, so easy with the big words," said Travis giving Rishi a skewed, playful look.

"Who knows you could be next in line of famous dropouts like Bill Gates or Mark Zuckerberg," said Rishi.

"Didn't actually drop out, maybe that's the problem."

"Don't worry, do your effort as best as you can. Success follows excellence," said Rishi.

"Counting on it." Travis bobbed his head vigorously.

"All right, okay, let's say persistent in maturing perspectives," said Rishi. "Maturing our perspectives allows us to lead better lives because it saves us from being whipsawed by the circumstances. But the real benefit is that it pulls our mind back from the frenzy and craziness of this world, allows us to become calmer and peaceful. It sets the stage."

"Okay," said Travis. "Then what?"

"The third step of the spiritual path, quieting your mind and ego progressively. There are many techniques for calming your mind, including the most powerful one — meditation."

"I want to learn all about meditation," said Travis.

"Sure, I'll share with you what I know."

"I can't wait," said Travis.

"I appreciate your enthusiasm," said Rishi. "Thanks."

Travis looked down, his fingers interlocked with the tip of his thumbs touching each other. He moved the tips around each other. "You said the cycle feeds on itself?"

"Yes. Transforming your thoughts and maturing your perspectives helps in quieting the mind, which allows the soul to shine through. Because you experience glimpses of peace, it allows you to step back from the world and further allows the transformation of your thoughts and the maturing of your perspectives. This, in turn, feeds the mind's calmness."

"Like a whirlpool."

"Yes," said Rishi.

"Why do you say bit by bit, why can't it be bang, quiet your mind and overnight infinite happiness?" said Travis.

Rishi sneered. "In the age of the internet, we want everything instantaneously."

"Well, why not?" Travis tapped his thumb.

"Think of it this way, we're all 200 pounds overweight, and it's taken us thirty years to accumulate all that weight. Even if we work non-stop in the gym, we can't lose all that weight in a weekend. It'll take months if not years of sweat and pain."

"It'll take a lot of effort and persistence," said Travis.

"That's the challenge — to be persistent. Going to the gym every day forms a habit and your body begins to expect it. The whole thing then feeds on itself. After months and years, slowly but surely all those layers of excess weight wear off and finally, a new you emerges," said Rishi.

Travis grinned. "Fit and trim like me."

"Yes, like you. A few years back, I put on weight. Suchi wouldn't ask me how long I was on the treadmill, she'd only ask if I was on it. She wanted to make sure I didn't break the habit. If you break a habit, it's difficult to get back in the rhythm."

"You got that right," said Travis.

"Similarly, our mind has layers and layers of memories, emotions, and thoughts," said Rishi. "Only when we're able to withdraw from those layers will we experience our soul. The thick cocoon of our mind wraps our soul. Only when the cocoon dissolves can the beautiful butterfly emerge and spread its colorful wings. That can take a long time and a lot of work."

"Stay persistent and be regular," said Travis.

"That's extremely important, and no expectations."

Travis winced. "No expectations?"

"Yes. Any expectations about wanting infinite happiness will prevent your mind from calming down. Your expectations will always be waiting, wanting to peek around the corner. If your mind keeps resurfacing, it'll disturb the stillness. Benchmarks, comparisons, and expectations drive every pursuit in the material world, but when you pursue spirituality, have zero expectations. Do it just for the sake of doing it."

"You sold me on the ultimate happiness and now you're saying don't focus on the goal," said Travis.

Rishi's eyes twinkled as he smiled. "You're pretty smart. That's exactly what I'm saying. To get your mind interested in the spiritual path, I've to describe the reward, but if your mind craves the reward then you're doomed."

"So it's a bait and switch," said Travis.

Rishi frowned. "It's not. If you can't walk, you need crutches. It's just a tool. But once you start walking, you've to discard the tool. It's not bait and switch. Everything has a utility value. Use it beyond its utility value and it becomes a burden. Similarly, the mind is a crutch —"

"A crutch?" Travis tilted his head. "Seriously?"

"Yes, it's a tool, we need it to get started and help us stay focused on the spiritual path. But once on the path, the mind must be dormant, otherwise, it'll interfere with our progress."

Travis looked unsure.

"If you want to sleep, you need your mind to turn off the TV, wear comfortable clothes, dim the lights and adjust the pillow. After that point, you don't need the mind. If you keep the mind active thinking about how you can fall asleep faster you're not going to fall asleep," said Rishi.

Travis nodded.

"Don't keep expectations about how fast you'll find peace, don't fantasize about experiencing infinite happiness, otherwise the mind will become overactive and crash the party."

"Okay, I won't," said Travis.

"And, don't compare your spiritual progress with anyone else. If you ask someone what he, she experiences, or what stage he or she is in, it'll make you either unhappy or happy. Don't fall into that trap. Pursue spirituality just for its own sake, without reference to anything, any timeline, or anyone else."

"Don't compare, and no expectations." Travis thrust his fist downwards on the sofa. "Will that be difficult?"

"Not if you go with the flow."

"Flowwww with the river," said Travis in a lyrical manner, mimicking Rishi's accent, and swaying his hand.

Rishi smiled. "Yes, go with the flow."

"I need to understand what you mean by flow," said Travis.

"You will." Rishi smiled broadly.

"What?" said Travis.

"I'm excited," said Rishi.

"I can see that," said Travis. "But why?"

"Some of the aspects of spirituality are so beautiful. Even just thinking about it makes me happy."

"Well, then share it, I can't wait," said Travis.

"Me neither, but, before we do that, some more coffee?"

"Sure," said Travis.

They both got up. Rishi refilled Travis' coffee at the bar and refilled his water. He pointed to a bowl of grapes and offered it to Travis who declined instead reaching for a cereal bar. Rishi broke off a bunch, put in a bowl, and grabbed an empty bowl. Travis finished the cereal bar and they walked back. Travis helped carry the extra bowl. He stepped aside for a minute to check his emails and text messages.

Experience your soul,
it is the ultimate purpose of your life!

Start your spiritual journey today.
Spirituality is within your reach.

Chapter 8: Spirituality is Natural

Rishi made himself comfortable by placing one of the smaller pillows behind his lower back. Making a cascading gesture, Rishi said, "Spirituality's as natural as a river flowing downstream. Just relax and let nature do its work. It's absolutely beautiful how it works." He pressed his right-hand fingers together to form a cone and pressed it against his chest. "Spirituality is inborn in us and it's completely natural."

"Is it really natural?"

"Yes, just like every human…," Rishi paused to search for an example, "…has the ability to float, the ability to swim."

"Only if they're able-bodied," said Travis.

> *Spirituality is inborn in us and it is completely natural.*

"Yeah, okay," said Rishi dismissive of the technical point. "Swimming is inherent in us. Babies and kids can learn swimming easily, adults, on the other hand, can develop the fear of water. Look at me, I don't know how to swim."

"You don't!" Travis giggled.

Rishi gave Travis a dirty look as he smiled. "I did try to learn. Suchi enrolled me, but after six months the swimming instructor came and said I was giving the school a bad name."

Travis laughed. "No, they didn't."

Rishi laughed too. "Priya was young, she told me, 'Dad, it's three feet of water, if you feel scared just stand up.'" Rishi laughed in his characteristic loud laugh. He caressed his forehead. "Oh, my."

"Funny," said Travis still laughing.

"I know. In any case, this is a great point. I have the ability to swim, it's been there since the day I was born. I know it intellectually, know it conceptually, and yet my mind can't overcome the fear of putting my head below the water."

We are wired from birth to make spiritual progress.

"It's not that bad," said Travis.

"I know, but I'd stand there looking at the water. My trainer would say, 'Stop analyzing the water, just dive in.' My mind was the stumbling block and stopped me from accessing my natural swimming ability."

"Spirituality is our natural ability, yet our mind prevents us," said Travis.

"Perfectly stated! You're gifted from birth with spiritual ability, it's automatically available to you."

"Automatically?" asked Travis.

"Yes, you don't have to holler to the soul, don't have to stand upside down on your head. Think about this way. The landscape becomes visible when the fog lifts, no effort is required to produce the landscape. It doesn't go anywhere, it doesn't come back. Similarly, our soul's always there."

"Good analogy. Easy to understand," said Travis.

Rishi took a bow. "Our constant storm of thoughts and emotions never allows our mental fog to lift. Whenever this mental fog lifts, the soul becomes evident by itself. That's why this is the most natural process. Spirituality is as natural as swimming. Don't let anyone else tell you otherwise."

"I like that it's natural. That's cool."

Rishi broke off a few grapes. He eyed each grape, playing with them between his fingers and eating them one by one. "Most things in nature are, that's what's fascinating. If you put a seed in the soil and water it regularly, it'll grow naturally into a plant. If you workout regularly your muscles will develop naturally. As we quiet our minds, our metaphorical spiritual muscles develop naturally."

As his mind processed Rishi's discussion, Travis looked down at the silk rug. The intricate design of flowers and endlessly curving branches caught his eye. "You've explained spirituality as simple and natural — " Rishi began to speak, but Travis continued, "then why's spirituality made out to be so complicated. Why's — "

"Why's it complex when described by others?" said Rishi.

"Yup, this rug," Travis pointed downwards, "the design's complex, but it doesn't look complex. Is that what you've done, made complex simple? In the online articles I read, spirituality's not as simple nor natural."

Rishi leaned forward. "Are you trying to second guess me?" said Rishi trying to be funny, but it did not come across as such.

"No," said Travis in a serious tone. "It wasn't just complicated, but even unattainable. Not for ordinary people."

Rishi smiled knowingly. "It's complicated because humans like to overcomplicate."

"Overcomplicate how?" asked Travis.

"Let me think of an analogy —"

"Love your analogies," said Travis.

Rishi smiled. "Ever eaten a mango?"

"In salads."

"Mangoes were first grown in India several thousand years ago," said Rishi. "People there are crazy about mangoes, incredibly delicious with great health benefits. Mmm, mmm."

"You're drooling."

Rishi licked his lips and laughed. "The point is we can simply eat a ripe mango and enjoy it tremendoooously."

Travis smiled. "Okay."

"Today, thousands of chef's use mangoes in their recipe. In India, they use them in chutney, in Mexico, salsas, in America, salads. Chefs dissect every aspect of the mango. How sweet it needs to be, when to eat it ripe, how to use it raw in recipes, what size, what color, how to freeze it. Some will even sell you a mango flavored drink with no benefits of an actual mango."

"I know, disgusting," said Travis. "So your point is a simple mango became distorted, commercialized... complicated."

"Yes, we could've simply enjoyed the mango, but now we've studied, cooked and consumed it in a million ways," said Rishi. "Those ways are valid because our minds crave variety."

"Done the same with spirituality," said Travis, "there are thousands of religious ways."

"Yes, people have colored spirituality by their intellectual capacity, region, culture, faith, and the societal norms of the times in which they lived." Rishi pressed his right and left fingertips against each other. "They've overwhelmed and obscured the essence of spirituality. There's so much beauty in the pursuit of spirituality. We can enjoy it without needing a million different rituals and interpretations," said Rishi.

Rishi paused and let his body relax. "Spirituality doesn't need fanfare — spirituality is simple — spirituality is natural."

Rishi felt harmonious, his words were coming out as if he was channeling the greatest wisdom in the Universe. In awe of his own words, he had a satisfied look on his face. He was listening to his words, reaffirming to himself the wisdom of his own words. He was both the orator and the audience.

"So, ignore what everyone else is saying?" asked Travis.

"And what, have all confidence in me?"

Travis feigned a frown and rolled his eyes. "Not doubting you," said Travis, "just want to be sure."

Rishi raised his palms halfway. "I know, I know. Let me share two examples of simple solutions related to my health."

"Okay," said Travis a tad intrigued.

"I've found a way to kill my throat infections."

"How?"

"Do you know ginger?" asked Rishi.

"Yup, ginger root."

"As soon as I develop a cold and an irritation in the throat or a cough, I immediately cut a small piece of ginger, peel it, and put it in my mouth. Ginger's extremely pungent, so even if you bite into it a little, it feels as if your mouth is burning."

"Really!"

"Yeah, but that's good. Ginger is a natural anti-viral, anti-bacterial agent. Because it's so pungent, I suspect the bugs die on contact as the ginger juice flows down your throat."

"Does it work?" asked Travis.

"Like a charm. I take it three times a day, and it kills the infection within 24 hours," said Rishi.

"I should try that next time," said Travis.

"You can take antibiotics or cough syrups, but they take their time and to me aren't as effective. Just a disclaimer here, what worked for me may not work for you," said Rishi. "Plus, be careful how much ginger you consume, it can do a number on your stomach if you consume too much."

"Thanks for the disclaimer, Mr. Lawyer," said Travis shaking his torso. "Don't worry, I'll be careful."

"Good." Rishi put the branches of grape in the empty bowl. "Let me share the other example."

"Okay."

"Fifteen years ago, I used to suffer from severe heartburn. A doctor prescribed an acid-reducing drug, but it didn't help."

"What did you do?"

"A doctor in India gave me a simple solution. Never to drink water or any fluid when I was hungry. When you're hungry, your body produces acid in anticipation. I suspect when you add any fluid at that time, it causes the acidic liquid to rise and enter your esophagus. That irritation in the esophagus causes heartburn."

"Never a good idea to add water to an acid," said Travis reciting a Chemistry lesson. "So you stopped drinking water?"

Rishi laughed. "Not completely. I did stop drinking fluids before and during meals. I drink thirty minutes after I've eaten. Whenever I get hungry during non-meal times, I find something to eat, ideally a piece of fruit. Saliva is alkaline so when you eat something it helps neutralize the acid."

"This solved your acidity?" asked Travis.

"Took three months, I had to change my lifestyle to eat my meals at regular times, add more fruits and raw vegetables to my diet. I started drinking water with lemon in it. Once the esophagus lining healed, I felt great. I have stayed with that lifestyle and for fifteen years, it has worked. It does flare up sometimes, but it's because I become careless. Then, I focus back on the basics and it goes back into control."

"Wow. Heartburn's a multi-billion dollar industry!"

"Yeah, I know," gulped Rishi. "Just a simple solution solved my problem, and I can ignore all the pharmaceutical drugs. I'm not a doctor to tell you if it'll work for everyone, but it worked for me. Should I rely on an expensive drug that was not helping me just because billions were spent on developing it, or should I listen to the seemingly simple solutions that worked for me?"

"Go with what works for you." Travis tapped his thumb.

"There you have it. We can focus on all the scriptures, numerous religious doctrines, all the religious interpretations, or we can go with the simple solution that works for us."

Travis opened his eyes wide and smiled. "No argument here. I loved your natural remedies. I'm going to try them. Thank you for sharing them buddy."

Rishi closed his eyes. "Thank you, Travis. You mean a lot to me. Your listening to me, your encouragement means a lot to me. It gives me greater confidence."

"Are you kidding me? This is helping me so much! Watching you in peace is making me peaceful, which is exactly what I was hoping. So, thank you!"

Rishi smiled lightly. Both men were lucky to have each other. They both were progressing at the conscious and the subconscious levels. Talking with someone who listens without judgment is such a gift, and finding someone who is a genuine guide and guru is truly a blessed event.

Rishi turned sober. "I'll admit to you, sometimes I doubt myself and wonder if I could be dead wrong about my spiritual path and pursuit."

"Come, on, Rishi." Travis shook his head dismissively.

"No, I'm serious," said Rishi. "It's a serious burden. What gives me confidence is when I see the stuff work. When I experience peace, and I'm a terrible person —"

"You're not. Why would you say that?" said Travis.

Rishi shook his head and looked away. "...My point is if I can experience moments of bliss, then anyone can. I just want to share that. I just wanna share that."

"And, bless you for that!" said Travis.

Rishi bowed. "So many religious leaders pass verdict on people and tell us spirituality is out of our reach. I want to change that misguided, and frankly, harmful thinking. I want to discuss that point next. What I'm going to share goes against conventional thinking, and I realize that message is going to be shocking for many."

"Well, don't worry about that. You're among friends."

"Shocking it may be, but it helps us move forward in our spiritual journey," said Rishi.

Spirituality is as intrinsic to us as our breath.

Spirituality is as natural as a seed growing up to be a plant.

Chapter 9: Spirituality Does Not Discriminate!

Travis asked, "To pursue spirituality do we have to move to a monastery?"

Rishi shook his head. "That's like saying you can read only if you go to the library. A library is highly conducive because everyone is reading, but it isn't a necessity. Some people go to the library, yet they don't read because they spend time on their phone. You can read just as fine at home if you focus. You can achieve spiritual awakening in your home!"

> *You can achieve spiritual awakening in your home!*

Travis eyed Rishi. "We don't have to become monks?"

"Listen, monks do have a leg up. But your soul and a monk's soul is the same energy. You can, living your daily life, achieve spirituality just as well."

Travis pointed to himself. "Ordinary people can do it?"

"Yes, spirituality isn't an exclusive club." Rishi stretched his hands out. "It's available to every person on Earth without any preconditions. An emperor and a cobbler, a president and a soldier, a super-intelligent and a less-intelligent person, everyone regardless of their life's condition has the same spiritual ability. People who have a comfortable living with all the amenities of life can experience spirituality without sacrificing those comforts."

"I like that!" said Travis feeling the couch.

"Me too," said Rishi, as he gestured gently with his hand. With a mischievous grin he added, "A broker on Wall Street and a lawyer on Main Street, even they can achieve spirituality."

"Oh, no, them too?" Travis chuckled.

True peace and bliss is attainable not just by monks and ascetics, we all, living our daily lives, can achieve that Ultimate Happiness.

Rishi laughed. "Yeah, them too. And, further, people who are religious and atheists, both can achieve spirituality."

Travis squirmed.

Rishi did a wave with his hand. "The ability to swim has been there in us since we were born. No one can impart it to us or take it away. Similarly, no one can impart or take away our spiritual ability!" Rishi's eyes shone with a mesmerizing quality.

Our spiritual ability is unaffected by our beliefs, whether we are religious or atheist!

"Really?" asked Travis. "How can atheists be spiritual?" How would they have spiritual capability?"

"That's the amazing beauty of spirituality!"

"What's the beauty?" asked Travis.

"Spirituality does not discriminate. It cannot!" said Rishi, making a declaration that will reverberate through the annals of time.

Taken aback by the declaration and Rishi's steely confidence in making the declaration, Travis repeated the declaration, letting it digest and probing it at the same time, "Spirituality does not discriminate." Travis brushed his hair aside. "Boy, this is a big one... I know people say they're spiritual and not religious, but I've always seen it intertwined. I've to get used to the idea that atheists too have spiritual ability."

Spirituality does not discriminate. It cannot!

Rishi smiled. "Listen, spirituality is not a club exclusive to followers of one religion. It's available to all including someone living in the Amazon rainforest who has never come across organized religion and the modern world. Spirituality is there in him as much as it is in you or me."

"I need time to digest this," said Travis, "...actually, you know what, there are days when I'm a borderline atheist, and I still believe I can be spiritual. So, maybe it doesn't matter whether you're an atheist or religious," Travis scanned the floor, "then is it our temptations and vices that decide if we can be spiritual?"

Rishi grimaced. "Temptations and vices are judgmental words, influenced by society's norms. In India, pre-marital sex was a no-no, especially for girls. An unimaginable sin! When I came to the US, pre-marital sex didn't seem to carry the same level of stigma, at least in the TV shows."

Travis smiled coyly.

"Polygamous relationships are unacceptable in the US, but okay in the Middle East," said Rishi. "In the past, US society was uncomfortable with homosexuality and many described it as sinful, an act against nature, but now views are changing."

"Even Pope Francis said, 'Who am I to judge gays?'"

Rishi pressed his thumb. "Every society chooses its values and evolves them over time. The definition of vices is influenced by societal norms and acceptable practices. Society expects you to follow its values, otherwise, it can make your life uncomfortable."

"I think I see where you're going with this," said Travis.

"Do you?" said Rishi. "These norms and traditions, these temptations and vices have little to do with spirituality. Whether you had pre-marital sex, how many wives or husbands you have or had, whether you're hetero, homo, or bisexual, asexual or hypersexual, may or may not be acceptable based on your society's values, but all of that does not affect whether you're eligible to experience infinite happiness."

Travis widened his eyes. "It doesn't?"

"No! Your body is male, female or transgender. Your mind is hetero or homosexual. But, your soul doesn't have a sexual designation. Infinite happiness has to do with your soul, not with

Our spiritual ability is unaffected by our deeds and shortcomings.

your mind or body. Your mind and body can't ever taint your soul. Your soul is pure — it can only be pure!"

Travis smiled. "I like the part about the soul being pure." He analyzed further. "Okay, vices are defined by society, but I bet, people have to be good to be spiritual, bad people can't —"

Like a coach helping a student with a Math problem, Rishi intervened, "You could be a person with good or bad deeds, you could have shortcomings, doubts, and false beliefs. None of it makes a difference. Spirituality does not care! Just because you harm someone, your soul doesn't leave you," Rishi opened and closed his fist, "it still functions in you."

"Whoa, that's dangerous," said Travis almost jumping up. "Don't have to be a good, decent human being? You gotta be kidding me! Don't believe that, not for a second."

Anticipating a pushback, Rishi watched Travis's spirited pushback with amusement. He let Travis continue.

"Every religion says you must be a good person to be in communion with God. They wrong? Is morality not important? Might as well sell me some snake oil," said Travis walking close to the edge of the disagreement precipice.

"Excuse me! Snake oil my foot!" said Rishi fighting like a champion boxer defending his title. He and Travis had a long history of pushing each other when they worked together.

Travis laughed, seeing Rishi in his characteristic feisty form. It brought back memories. Rishi laughed too.

"Surely, we need to be nice to become spiritual?" said Travis. "What you're saying is we don't have to be good?"

"No, no." Rishi shook his head. "That's not what I'm saying at all. See how things get misinterpreted."

Travis folded his arms. "That's exactly what you said."

"Not at all," said Rishi wagging his forefinger with a little urgency. "If you harm someone you'll definitely pay a price for it, there's no escape for it. That is a law of the Universe, and a law of society, you must and will pay for your deeds."

"Very good, I agree with that." Travis gave a firm nod.

"Wait, I'm not done. There are two dimensions — the material and the spiritual world. They're both parallel dimensions of this Universe. What you do in the material world stays in the material world. The spiritual world can never ever be touched or tainted by the material world," said Rishi.

"What you do in Las Vegas stays in Las Vegas," said Travis with a little impatience and a little sarcasm.

Rishi's face sobered as he remembered an incident, but Travis did not notice. Rishi said, "Your deeds are committed in the material world and the rewards and punishments will be administered in this world. If you get a speeding ticket in California, Texas won't prosecute you, California will."

"There is no hell and heaven?" Travis threw his fingers up.

"There's absolutely a hell and heaven — but it's here in the material world — on Earth," said Rishi. "Have you seen the excruciating pain and exhilarating pleasures that exist on Earth? What we sow we reap — here. It's all in this dimension."

Travis looked away, doing his best to concur but still wrestling with the idea.

"Listen, the soul is pure energy. It's independent of your deeds!" said Rishi. "Your TV displays both a serene lake and a violent volcano. But neither affect the TV, it doesn't become wet or hot. Similarly, your soul is unaffected by your deeds."

"Soul is independent of our deeds, our sins? Really!"

Rishi lifted his fingers slightly. "Even a murderer could make spiritual progress if he decided that's what he wants, and worked hard on it," said Rishi doubling down on the point and pushing into an even more controversial space.

"Whaaaat?" Travis ruffled his hair.

"It's true," said Rishi raising his palm, unrelenting and un-swayed by Travis's outburst.

"Uh, uh, not gonna convince me of that." Travis animated-ly waved his finger.

"I know, I realize that but before you get riled up, breathe a little, and be open-minded."

"I'm open," said Travis, smirking a little bit. "I bought your two parallel dimensions. A killer! That's way off. You better re-think this."

"Okay," said Rishi in a serious tone, recognizing he was presenting a difficult point. "Deeds and actions, your character, your behavior and conduct are all connected to?"

Travis shrugged. "Don't know."

"Think… it's easy, you know the answer," said Rishi.

"The mind?" answered Travis.

"Exactly, so we don't really have a pious person or a killer person, we have a pious mind or a killer mind. A saint's mind is pure and kind, a murderer's mind is troubled and angry."

Travis tapped his thumb. "Yeah, so?"

"A killer's mind will be troubled and agitated, it'll have great difficulty in becoming peaceful. If you're mean to others, your mind will struggle to calm down. Bad deeds, jealousy, greed, fear, anger, and addiction to sensory pleasures agitate your mind at the conscious and the subconscious level. A pious mind, which does good deeds, is helpful and kind is certainly more able to quiet itself and migrate toward the path of spiritu-ality. Good deeds make your mind peaceful."

"Okay, see now you're saying the right things," said Travis.

Rishi smiled. "But it's not guaranteed. Even a pious person has to work hard to quiet their mind. Many priests have doubts about their faiths, but they never raise them because they're afraid of how society may perceive them. Such fear is their nemesis. They have sexual and other worldly desires, which they suppress because they're afraid of losing their religious denomination. You can spend all your life serving a religious order, but if you live with fear, doubt, and denial, you will stunt your spiritual progress. If their mind is agitated, if they don't calm their mind they'll never make spiritual progress."

Travis digested silently, letting Rishi make his case.

"On the flip side," said Rishi, "murderers are least likely to seek spirituality. But, if they stop living in the past, change their personality, and completely quiet their minds, they will experience their soul. Unlikely, but absolutely possible."

Travis shook his head, not buying it. He moved the pillows away to give himself some extra room, almost, as if he was readying himself to spring up. "The murderer example, is that realistic or just for over-dramatization?"

"Me over-dramatize?" joked Rishi but Travis did not smile.

Travis's breathing became faster, "You're saying we can be killers and still find peace."

"No, no, that's the opposite interpretation," said Rishi. "Let me try again. There are so many historical stories of bad people who turned their lives around and walked the path of righteousness. You'll hear about killers who make a genuine transformation in their lives. They're still executed for their crimes, the law doesn't let them go free, but they achieve peace while in prison waiting for their death sentence to be executed."

Travis looked down at the rug. "Every saint has a past, every sinner has a future."

"I'm sorry, what?" said Rishi.

Travis looked up. "Haven't you heard that quote?"

"No, I haven't," said Rishi.

"It means sinners can redeem themselves, and no saint started as a perfect human being," explained Travis.

"No saint is done until they experience their soul," said Rishi. "Spirituality is our final evolution step."

"I should change the quote." Travis waved his hand. "Saints and sinners both have a future."

"That's nice," said Rishi, happy Travis was seeing the point.

Travis had not made the turn though. He puffed at his hair. "Killers becoming fully spiritual, how can it be allowed in this Universe of yours?" He jabbed a finger toward Rishi.

"Water does not discriminate," said Rishi in a comforting tone a grandfather would use with his grandson. "Whether it's a saint or a killer, water works to keep both afloat."

Travis smiled a little at Rishi's analogy.

"The law of its own nature binds water," said Rishi. "It must float all objects that lie in water. If a saint and a killer lie still in the water, they'll float alike. If they know swimming, they'll be able to swim equally well. Their deeds have no consequence to water."

"True," said Travis.

Rishi paused to process a thought. "And, I'm talking about the physical world, not the miracle world where mythological figures walk on water and break the laws of Physics. This is not a faith-based discussion. This is a can-I-convince-myself-of-the-logic discussion. You with me?" said Rishi.

"Yup, okay… water is impartial and bound by its law."

"Like water, our soul is also governed by the laws of the Universe and its own nature. I'll share another example."

"Please," said Travis with a slight smile.

"Think of a steel foundry," said Rishi. "Sometimes you melt pure iron rods in perfect condition to make steel. At other times, you have corroded iron rods, scrappy and flaky. Makes no difference to the foundry. It will melt both rods alike."

"Okay."

"The real magic is in the alloying elements that turn iron into steel," said Rishi. "Once iron turns into steel, it can never rust again, water can do no harm to it."

Travis nodded.

"What was before doesn't matter," said Rishi, "it could be virgin iron ore, a manufactured brand new iron rod, or a rusted piece of iron — all of it is transformed to steel."

Travis smiled. "Spirituality is the alloying element in our lives."

"Yes," said Rishi with a serious look, "whether we're pure as monks, or corroded as killers, once

> *Spirituality is the alloying element that makes our life perfect.*

we're melted and spirituality's mixed in, we become like steel. Not only will the past be meaningless, in the future, the material world won't be able to corrode us. We'll be able to mingle in the world, enjoy it, serve it selflessly, live out our lives, and yet we'll be unaffected by it. We'll be strong as steel and blissful forever."

"So, that's our purpose in life — become spiritual steel," said Travis tongue-in-cheek.

"Yes. I like that," said Rishi as he smiled. Travis smiled too.

Encouraged, Rishi added, "Take a lighted bulb which is covered with a thick piece of cloth. When you uncover the bulb, the light will shine through because it has no choice. It must. Whether the bulb was covered with a rich beautiful cloth or an ugly cloth, once you remove it, the light will emerge."

"The light is always there, once the cloth is removed it must come out," said Travis.

"Yes! Light is bound by its nature. It can't say an ugly rag was covering me, so I won't shine through. Cool example?" Rishi leaned back as if he had made his case. He was satisfied.

"Yup, I get it," Travis nodded. "Whether you're a killer or a saint, if you quiet your mind, your soul will become visible."

Rishi clapped. "Yes, the soul will shine through. It has no choice, it must shine through naturally and automatically," said Rishi sharing the grandest of all spiritual knowledge.

If the fog of your mind lifts, your soul will shine through automatically. It must!

"That's actually quite powerful," said Travis with his eyes lightening up. He pushed his head ever so slightly toward Rishi.

Rishi was still dwelling in the satisfaction of having made a difficult point. He closed his eyes and recited, "Quiet your hungry mind, and your happy soul will shine through!"

"I understand your muntruh now," said Travis in a sincere tone. "It's making sense."

Rishi smiled. "Good, as we discuss more, you'll appreciate it even more. Let's talk more about deeds. Is there a way for a high school student to escape his failing grade?"

"Nope. How?" said Travis.

"By not going to school anymore," said Rishi.

"Uh, uh, against the law, at least in Texas. My mother always reminded me, if I skipped school, I'd have to explain it to a judge," said Travis.

"As long as you live in Texas, the law applies," said Rishi.

"Where are you going with this?" asked Travis.

"If you move to a remote island... say, named, Paradise Island, somewhere in the Indian Ocean, then the Texas law doesn't apply." Rishi waved his hand with a flair. "You can be in bliss on Paradise Island. Since there are no schools your Texas school grades and detention record won't matter."

"I... how does that...?"

"This material world is like your school," said Rishi. "As long as you're in school, the grades matter. But if you leave the material world and enter the blissful, spiritual world, your deeds and so-called sins from the material world don't apply."

"Well...," said Travis as he absorbed the logic.

"Now if you come back to Texas, you'll be required to reenlist in school, and they'll have your past records. If you stay on Paradise Island, you're unaffected by your school record."

"Paradise Island, here I come." Travis gestured a flight.

"Do you know why our deeds affect us only in the material world?" asked Rishi.

Travis raised his eyebrows and shook his head.

Rishi touched his forehead. "It's because our mind carries out the deeds, and therefore only it can and must suffer the consequences. Our soul is independent of the deeds and its consequences. Once you experience the soul, the mind becomes irrelevant. Our mind is the bouncer, but once we're inside and meet our pop star, the bouncer doesn't matter."

"That... makes sense," said Travis. "While I was at Ixsor, I was always worried about my poor performance reviews, but once I started Travisto, I was free. Actually, a better example would be if I'd become a movie star, then my previous work and performance reviews would have zero relevance. I think my example is better than your Paradise Island example."

"You know what," Rishi smiled, "you're right."

Travis grinned.

Rishi raised his index finger. "Those who achieve infinite happiness by connecting with the spiritual world become impervious to the material world. Spirituality redeems them. Their past deeds and the resulting rewards or punishments become immaterial to them. Fame and fortune don't affect them. They rise above sadness and happiness, pain and pleasure, insults and praise. They become free from the material world even though they interact with it. They may live and act in the world, but they do so selflessly. They become the true servants of people while transfixed in their blissful state."

"That sounds so good," said Travis.

Rishi said, "Throughout history, there are stories about prophets who showed no animosity toward their tormentors because they had transcended the material world. They were in constant bliss no matter what the circumstance and how much pain they were suffering. The material world has a hold on us only until we experience the soul in its full glory!"

Travis raised his eyebrows. "That's incredible."

Rishi said, "People living ordinary and imperfect lives can achieve spirituality. Spirituality is our true redemption. Spirituality is our birthright! Spirituality is our destiny!"

Travis smiled with satisfaction. "Spirituality is our destiny!"

"Yes, it is," said Rishi. "The Universe is constantly encouraging us, that's why every human being has a spiritual beckoning. It's in our wiring. That's how the Universe designed us. We can and must graduate from the material world to the spiritual world. That is our evolutionary path. This is a powerful, powerful message for you, me, and for all humans. Everyone must take this seriously and progress spiritually."

> *Spirituality is your birthright!*
> *Spirituality is your destiny!*

"I like that very much," said Travis.

"If you like that, you'll love what we discuss next. It's the question people have been asking for thousands of years!"

> *Nothing can deny us our human-ness, and nothing can deny us our spiritual-ness!*
>
> *All of us have equal access to spiritual ability — regardless of race, gender, sexual identity, deeds, intelligence, and status.*
>
> *Graduate from the material world to the spiritual world. It is your evolutionary goal!*

Chapter 10: Can we "See" God?

Displaying the excitement of a performer about to amaze his audience, Rishi asked, "You ready for the big question?"

"Sure," said Travis picking up his excitement.

"Do you know anyone who's seen, God?" asked Rishi.

Travis looked sideways not sure of an answer.

"You know no one who's reported meeting God?" pressed Rishi.

Travis struggled. "Nope," he said a little exasperated.

"Think about it," said Rishi. "Imagine if someone was to meet God, how big a news would that be?"

"Huuuuge!" said Travis.

"People portray God as living behind the clouds, in space," said Rishi. "We know there's just galaxies in space, no physical evidence of God. Question is — why can't we see Him? Why haven't we met Him?" said Rishi with the flair of a prosecutor in court.

"I'll be darned, never thought about it," said Travis. "If I meet Him, I do have a few questions for Him," said Travis.

"We all do!" said Rishi.

"Okay, so where's He? Why can't we see Him?" asked Travis, turning back the question.

"I'll tell you. But first, let me share a few things. Say you've never been to see the Himalayas," said Rishi.

"I haven't," said Travis.

"If I'm in the Himalayas and I call you to describe the scene in the richest, most poetic language, will you have the same experience as seeing those beautiful peaks with your own eyes?"

"Nope," said Travis.

"Now, imagine I'm at the Justin Bieber concert. He's singing really well. Can you get a feel for how well he's singing if I just text you and you don't actually get to hear it."

"Nope, need my ears," said Travis.

"You need the sense of hearing," said Rishi. "If I'm eating a cheesecake and I send you a picture, can you experience it?"

"No," said Travis. "My tongue and the cheesecake must come in contact."

"You need the right sense, the right tool to experience things," said Rishi.

"I get that. And, your point is?" Travis looked inquiringly.

Rishi paused to build the suspense. He leaned forward. "What I'm about to tell you is one of the greatest philosophical points of all times and of all spiritual discussions."

"You do love to dramatize," blurted out Travis.

Rishi's expression turned less exuberant. Travis blinked his eyes. "I didn't mean to —"

"That's okay. I'm not dramatizing... over-dramatizing, this, in fact, is so important, it's the underpinning of man's spiritual journey. The more we understand this statement the more spiritual progress we'll make... real progress as opposed to getting caught up in misinformation."

"Okay, spill it, you're killing me."

"I will, I will," said Rishi with a smile. Speaking slowly and deliberately, Rishi pronounced, "Your mind is not the tool to experience God!" Rishi put his hands on his thighs and sat there as a king would sit on his throne, with an air of authority.

Travis processed the statement.

"Your mind is not the medium to see God," said Rishi. "No matter how much you try, you'll never see God through your mind."

"What's the issue with the mind?" asked Travis. "Why can't it see God?"

> *Your mind is the wrong tool to find God.*
> *You can never "see" God though your mind.*

"That's like asking why can't your eyes taste the pizza. Or, why can't your tongue hear? There are different instruments for different purposes. Your mind is an instrument to engage in the material world, not a tool for the spiritual world!"

Travis took a deep breath and looked at the staircase to gather his thought. "Umm...."

Rishi said, "People try to convince themselves they're seeing God, but they aren't because they're using their mind. You need the right sense to experience God."

Rishi sat up straight with an intense look. "In the field of spiritual science, this statement that we can't see God through our minds is as big as Albert Einstein's simple but most powerful Physics formula e=mc^2."

Travis stared blankly.

Rishi lifted his palms slightly. "You're probably thinking this man's full of himself."

Travis shook his head. "Noooo, not thinking that. Is it really that important?"

"It is!" said Rishi. "It's like discovering the atom is the building block of the entire universe or discovering the Earth is round." Rishi gestured with both hands. "Truly understanding the fact that our mind's not the right medium to meet God is monumental!"

Your mind is an instrument for you to engage in the material world. It is not a tool to access the spiritual world.

Travis widened his eyes.

Rishi raised his finger. "I wish more religious leaders would truly understood this spiritual truth so they wouldn't misguide themselves," raising his voice a little Rishi said, "and their congregations."

Travis looked askance. "If not the mind, what is the right sense?" mused Travis, asking the most significant question.

Rishi gestured wide with his hands and brought them together to touch his chest. "You can experience God — only through your soul! Your soul is the handshake, the conduit to God. The soul is the sense

You can experience God… only through your soul! Your soul is the handshake, the conduit to God.

to meet God. The soul is the natural way to meet God!" He closed his eyes.

Travis leaned back and then perched forward. He narrowed his eyebrows dissecting the proclamation. "But is soul really the sense to meet God?"

Gently moving his head in a rhythmic fashion as if he was listening to melodious music, Rishi said, "Experiencing our soul is experiencing God. Our soul is the spiritual, divine energy in us. God is the ultimate divine energy. When we experience the soul, we experience that infinite energy."

Travis analyzed carefully. "What if someone doesn't believe in God? Will they still experience God?"

"Ah, very nice, great question!" Rishi did a thumbs up. "Belief in God is not a necessary condition for experiencing God! Isn't that paradoxical?" Rishi smiled enjoying the play of philosophy. "You know why belief in God doesn't matter?"

Travis shrugged.

Rishi touched his forehead. "Remember, I said, God can't be seen through our minds."

Travis squinted not making the connection.

"Your beliefs reside where? In your mind," said Rishi. "Keep aside what your mind thinks and believes. Whether you believe in God is a matter of your mind, it makes no difference to your soul what your mind thinks."

Travis moved his hair aside. "Umm...."

Rishi said in a comforting tone, "Okay, let me explain. Imagine I come across a cheesecake reviewers say is incredibly delicious. I go taste it and realize it really is tasty. I message you a picture and tell you the cheesecake is delicious. You've not tasted it, so you may or may not believe me."

"Umm, okay, with you so far."

"However, once you come and taste it with your tongue, you also experience the cheesecake is delicious."

"Okay," said Travis.

"Your belief or non-belief does not affect the taste of the cheesecake," said Rishi.

"True," said Travis.

"If you had believed me, that wouldn't have changed your experience, and if you hadn't believed me that also wouldn't have changed your experience. Your tongue determines your actual experience. Beliefs become ineffective and immaterial in the presence of the actual experience. Their utility is over. Beliefs can't color the Truth!"

> *Whether you believe or not does not affect the Truth. Beliefs cannot color the Truth!*

Travis took a second. His face brightened. "Love that! I may or may not believe, but once I experience it I will know."

"Exactly. Your experience trumps any belief you might have," said Rishi.

Travis surmised, "If God is the truth, we'll experience Him through the soul, regardless of whether we believe in him or not. And, if God isn't the truth, we will find that out as well."

"Wow, the student has overtaken the teacher!" said Rishi loudly and proudly as he got up and extended his palm out for a high-five. Travis sprung to his feet and high-fived.

Sitting down Rishi said, "Isn't that an awesome point?"

"Yup, very cool," said Travis.

Rishi's face beamed with an intense glow. "When we experience our soul, that's our gateway to God. That's the only way, the only way to experience God. Every other way is fake, every other way is false."

"I would've never thought that every other way is false," said Travis.

"Every other way involves the mind. Your mind can try to describe God, it can think it understands and comprehends God, but it can never truly experience God. All the people who try to tell you what God is, or what God stands for, take it with a grain of salt because they likely haven't experienced Him. Even the best, most articulate description is woefully inadequate in describing Him. Don't rely on any description of God, instead experience Him!"

Do not rely on a description of God, instead "experience" Him!

"This a big deal?" Travis felt a combination of exhilaration and intimidation.

"It is huge!" Rishi widened his eyes.

Travis hesitated. "Is it —"

"Truth?" said Rishi.

Travis narrowed his eyebrows. "Yeah."

"Absolutely," said Rishi, "and when you experience it, you'll know for sure. Billions of human beings don't see God because they're seeking God through their minds. It'll never happen for them. That's why you never hear a report of anyone meeting God. They'll see an image on a potato or on a slice of bread, or a shape in the clouds, that's not serious. God is not an image on some piece of bread. That's just man's limited mind, trivializing God. The only and true experience of God is through the soul!"

"Can we lowly human beings truly experience this infinite divine energy?" asked Travis.

"Ah, good question. Yes, we can. You know, you have the ability to produce life. You need a member of the opposite sex, but together you can produce life. What a divine miracle!" Rishi threw open his palms. "The ability to create life is such a powerful, mind-boggling phenomenon!"

"That's true, but…"

"Such a big miracle happens with such ease," said Rishi. "In a similar manner, we all can access and connect with the infinite, connect with God. It is natural and achievable." Rishi's face lit up, he was enjoying the discussion.

"Anyone experienced that?" asked Travis.

"The true spiritual seekers, they have experienced Him," said Rishi waving his hand as if he knew them all and was proud of them. "Listen carefully to the ancient sages of India, listen to the prophets and messiahs born through the ages worldwide, listen to the self-realizers and the nirvana achievers, listen carefully to their words my friend. They're describing the God experience. They all experienced God through their souls."

Rishi slumped back into the sofa, relishing his own words, reliving a small part of the peace that the great seekers in history have experienced before him.

Rishi closed his eyes. "They're the truly blessed ones because they fulfilled the ultimate purpose of their human birth. They fulfilled it. How beautiful! How simple! Connecting with your personal spiritual energy is connecting with the all-encompassing collective spiritual energy we call God!"

Travis felt like someone who was watching the Super Bowl in the stadium for the first time. He could feel the rush, yet there was a feeling of separation because neither of the teams playing were from his city. Rishi, on the other hand, was experiencing the exhilaration of a home team victory. He could have been on cloud nine, at least that is how it seemed to Travis.

Squirming a little, Travis interjected, "Hate to ask this question, sort of like poking the bubble."

"That's no problem," Rishi did an ok sign, "ask without hesitation."

Emboldened, Travis asked a doozy, "Do you know if God really does exist?" He quickly followed with, "I don't mean to offend."

Rishi laughed. "No offense. I know energy exists, and if I define God as all the collective energy, then God exists."

"Yes, but…."

"Always a but," said Rishi.

Travis hesitated.

"I'm just teasing, go ahead," said Rishi.

"…Isn't that a convenient definition?" asked Travis.

Unperturbed, Rishi explained his logic, "Don't seek God, seek the Truth. If you find the Truth, you will find God. That Truth, whatever it is, I might call it God, and you might call it science or something else, doesn't matter, it will be the Truth and that's all that matters."

> *Do not Search for God!*
> *Search for the Truth!*

Travis did not find any holes in the logic.

"If you truly find infinite happiness." Rishi widened his eyes. "I mean really infinite, truly infinite happiness, will it matter if you call it the God experience or something else." He gestured with his palms facing upwards. "Enjoy and focus on experiencing the cheesecake, why get caught up in names. The name is not the truth. Maybe they call cheesecake by some other name in Greece or Italy. Who cares! Focus on the taste, focus on the experience, that's the truth. Focus on the Truth!"

Travis eased up, his body relaxed. "I like that, focus on the Truth. I really like that."

Raising his voice Rishi asserted, "God is the constant that never changes. Truth is the constant that never changes. Because it never changes, it'll always be there, untarnished, uneroded, and brand new eternally."

The definition intrigued Travis, a faint smile on his face.

Rishi paused and closed his eyes. "In my definition, Truth is God! God is Truth!" said Rishi not in his usual authoritative voice but demurely as if he himself was lost and in awe

Truth is God!

God is Truth!

of that statement. "If you find the Truth, you will find God. That's our search — for the Truth."

Travis beamed. He had finally heard something he could wholeheartedly accept. "People can call God by different names, imagine Him in different ways, that's okay, but the Truth is what we seek." Travis chanted, "Truth is God. God is Truth." Travis stopped to let the statement sink in his being and then said, "Love that! That's actually pretty darn good!"

"Truth is God. God is Truth," repeated Rishi lost in his zone. The statement had asserted itself and it seemed to Rishi to have taken over the room, maybe not just the room but had taken over the entire creation — the Universe itself.

Rishi closed his eyes, experiencing a glimpse of infinite space and time. An ecstatic feeling to leave the false, limited, changing identity and ego at the shore, and immerse in the ocean of the changeless and infinite.

Why cannot we immerse in the Universe, and dissolve our false and finite identities in the Infinite now? Why do we wait?

Rishi opened his eyes. "God isn't an easy topic to discuss in philosophical terms. Easy to discuss in religious or devotional terms."

"I'm cool with it now. I get it," said Travis.

"I have more thoughts on what is God. It's eye-opening and challenges current notions, but I don't want to jump into that right now. Let's finish the difficult discussion of our hungry mind, and then as a reward, I'll take you beyond the clouds to show you God in his full glory."

Travis wanted to stay something about Rishi's flair for dramatization but he let it pass. "All right, Mr. Spiritual Scientist, I'm really curious but I'll wait patiently to see God's full glory. You realize He and I aren't on the best of terms."

"I know," said Rishi soberly. He looked away toward the windows.

"So where does religion fit in all of this," asked Travis.

"You want to open Pandora's Box?" asked Rishi.

Travis smiled. "Might as well, why hold back now!"

You can never "see" God through your mind.
Your soul is the only channel to Him.

Do not search for God, search for the Truth.
If you find the Truth, you will find God!

Chapter 11: Spirituality Versus Religion

Rishi had a bemused look. "Religion's a tricky subject."

Travis squinted. "Why?"

"Deeply religious people don't see the distinction between God and their religion," said Rishi. "I've failed to make my case with them." He laughed. "It's above my pay grade."

Travis nodded slightly.

"God and religion are completely distinct entities," said Rishi. "Religions are just different paths leading to one God."

"I agree with you," said Travis. "No argument there."

"Religion's been misused to judge people, not help them find peace. Misused to make people fear God, not love Him."

Travis tapped his thumb. "Fear sells."

"God doesn't care which religion you follow, or if you're an atheist." Rishi's face turned crimson. "Anyone who says otherwise has misinterpreted God and is misguiding you."

> *God does not care which religion you follow or if you even follow one.*

Travis stomped his feet. "I'm with you, hundred percent!"

"Religion can mean a lot of different things," said Rishi. "Spirituality's about one thing, your spirit. At the risk of upsetting people —"

Travis chuckled. "Don't worry, you're way past that."

Rishi smiled. "Religion is the middleman —"

"Aren't you quite religious?" interjected Travis.

"I am. I believe in God. I pray regularly, I follow the religious traditions, but when it comes to my search for spirituality, I keep the two separate. To me, there's a big difference between mythology and philosophy."

Rishi gestured as if he was plucking something. "For my worldly pursuits, I need mythology, for my spiritual pursuits, I need philosophy. I'm heavily influenced by Hindu philosophy but I also have my independent thinking. I pursue spirituality based on logic, not faith. And, Hindu philosophy guides you to challenge the logic, which gives me great encouragement. In fact, the philosophy is devoid of any religious context. Nowhere does it bring up Hinduism or says be a good Hindu. It just discusses truths, I go out and test those truths and accept them only if it is the truth. What about you, I don't know how you feel about religion?"

"I'm a lot less religious," said Travis. "I attended church at times with my parents growing up, but we weren't religious."

"What about your wife?" asked Rishi.

"Neither is she. We didn't do Nathan's memorial service in a church, did it in the park where he played soccer. Had big, life-size pictures of him." Travis's face sobered.

Rishi felt subdued.

"I visited a church after Nathan," said Travis, "but it left me more disturbed, couldn't accept the fact that God…," Travis looked away, "…all I want is peace."

"Let's work on that peace," said Rishi in an upbeat tone to lift Travis's mood. "Religion's very helpful for many people, but spirituality is the ultimate source of bliss and contentment. Religion's a path to spirituality, and a majority of the people use that path, and that's good, but it's possible to go direct."

"Let's go direct," said Travis with a thumbs up.

"I don't want to believe in God," said Rishi, "I want to experience God, firsthand, so I know He is the Truth!"

"You said it, experience trumps belief!" said Travis.

Rishi did a thumbs up. "I'm not a religious scholar by any means, but sometimes I analyze sayings across religions. They're amazingly similar."

Travis looked on, seeking more information.

"In the Hindu scripture Bhugvud Geet, Lord Krishun says, I am the self in all beings, I am the absolute, I am the source of all spiritual and material worlds," said Rishi.

"Really?"

"Yeah," said Rishi. "Do you know in the Christian scriptures, what God says when Moses asked, 'Who shall I say has sent me?'"

"Yes... I think he says, 'I am.'"

"I am that I am!" Rishi waited for the words to resonate with the room. "In Sanskrit, there are two muntruhs, 'Tat tvam asi,' and 'So hum.' The first one states, 'That you are,' the second one states, 'I am.' It's the same concept separated across centuries and regions. I am. I am."

"I am," said Travis.

"How incredibly beautiful is that!" said Rishi touching his fingers to his thumb. "You could spend an entire lifetime contemplating those two simple words, I AM. Not I was, or I am now, or I will be. Just, I am. I am present in everything, I am everything." Rishi wiggled himself. "A vibration's going through me even as I say it. Just powerful, powerful!"

Travis watched in amazement as always. He said, "Jesus says, 'The kingdom of God is in you.'"

"Yes, Lord Christ is referring to the soul in us," Rishi raised his fingers slightly, "in fairness, that's my interpretation."

"Our soul is the kingdom of God," said Travis.

Rishi smiled. "That's right. Do you know the greeting Prophet Mohammed gave his followers to use when they greet each other? This is fundamental to Islam."

"No clue."

"Peace be upon you." Rishi repeated, "Peace be upon you. What've we been talking about?"

"Peace," replied Travis.

"Prophet Mohammed says, 'The greatest struggle is for the conquest of self.'" Rishi looked at Travis wide-eyed. "Isn't that incredible! That's what we've been talking about — spirituality is the conquest of the mind, so we can meet our self."

Travis was dazzled with all the religious tidbits.

Rishi took a deep breath. "Lord Buddha masterfully describes how desires are the cause of our misery, and has given the remedy for our hungry minds." Rishi raised his hand slightly. "As you listen to the God-realized souls you see the science of life so clearly. They're all saying the same thing."

"That's really cool." Travis thought about it. "So I'm a little confused. I agreed religion was a just path. Then you shared all the religious sayings. So is religion needed then?"

Rishi smiled. "Let me tell you where religion fits."

"Okay," said Travis.

"In the Bhugvud Geet, Lord Krishun describes four paths for progress toward spirituality. They are the four Yogs."

"Yogs? What's that?" asked Travis.

"Have you heard of Yoga?"

"Of course," said Travis.

"It's a mispronunciation. The Sanskrit word is yog, pronounced yog-uh. It means union. You know which kind?"

Travis shook his head.

Rishi interlocked his fingers. "It's the union between us and our souls. And the union of our souls with the supreme soul."

"Wow. Cool. I had no idea yoga, err, yog meant that."

"It does. The four yogs are Bhakti, Kuhrum, Gyan, and Dhyan. Bhakti means devotion, Kuhrum is action, Gyan is spiritual knowledge, and Dhyan means silent meditation."

As he stretched a finger with each name, Travis said, "Devotion, action, knowledge, and meditation."

Rishi watched in satisfaction. "Devotion is the path of faith. Most religions emphasize the path of faith. You believe in God and love Him. Includes all the religious worship ceremonies, devotional singing, and dancing that can give you a high."

"Pure devotion," said Travis.

"Yes. Next, the path of selfless action. Your kuhrum, again this word is mispronounced as karma by most people."

"Karma, as in fate?" said Travis.

"Well, kuhrum actually means your actions or deeds. Your deeds determine your future, therefore kuhrum has been mislabeled as fate. It's pronounced kuh-rum."

"Kuh-rum," said Travis.

"That's good," said Rishi. "Kuhrum Yog is the path of selfless action. You don't take any credit for the work you're doing. When all your actions and outcomes are in His name, when you're just a tool in his hands, then all your ego melts away."

"I like that, it appeals to me," said Travis.

"That's the point, we like one or more of these paths based on our personalities. Some like devotion, others selfless service. Mother Teresa is a great example of a Kuhrum yogi," said Rishi.

"Get it."

Rishi continued, "Gyan Yog, the path of spiritual knowledge, is the path of analysis, and contemplation on the scriptures and the key questions facing life. It is developing a perspective of discernment. For example, recognizing the world as impermanent and transient. This is the work of the spiritual seekers who want to figure out the truth through analysis, and reorienting their mind."

"Like our discussion today?" said Travis.

"Yes. And, finally, the fourth yog, Dhyan, is the path of silent meditation. When you meditate, the soul reveals itself bit by bit and eventually, you experience infinite bliss. Not only is Dhyan yog my favorite, to me it's the ultimate yog."

"Why?" Travis raised his eyebrows.

"Some sages believe you need components of all, devotion, action, knowledge, and meditation, to find bliss, to find God. They say people are a mixture of all of these four aspects and hence they need to pursue all paths in combination."

"What do you think?" asked Travis.

"Meditation is the ultimate path, the final yog to engage before the soul manifests in its full glory. Let me say this more strongly. All the devotion, all the self-less action, all the spiritual knowledge, analysis, and discernment, cannot help you feel your soul if you do not meditate! Without meditation you can never achieve self-realization, you can never meet God."

Feeling a little intimated, Travis did not offer a comment.

"You know why I just said that?" asked Rishi.

"Nope."

Rishi smiled as a master revealing great truths. His eyes glistening and his face glowing. "Devotion, selfless action, and spiritual knowledge are all meant for the mind. Meditation is the only yog that sidelines the mind. If you remember —"

"We must calm the mind, only then the soul will show."

Rishi thumped the sofa. "Exactly."

Travis said, "Devotion, action, and knowledge are for the purposes of the mind. But, meditation goes beyond the mind."

Rishi smiled with great pride. "You're a great student!"

Travis grinned.

In his characteristic style of repeating important points, Rishi said, "Devotion, selfless action, and spiritual knowledge are important ways to help bring the hungry mind under control. But, the crown jewel is deep, silent meditation, which negates and sublimes the mind completely. When that happens, then we become golden."

Rishi smiled with a deep level of satisfaction.

Travis closed his eyes and relaxed back on the sofa.

"Now, let me tell you the real difference between religion and spirituality," said Rishi.

"Okay," said Travis, excitement in his voice.

"Religion is only for the purpose of your mind. Religion has zero effect on your spirit. Ultimately, we must put religion aside to experience the spirit." Rishi smiled.

Travis nodded, "I figured as much."

"Let me give you an analogy."

"Oh, no." Travis grabbed his cheeks, feigning overload.

Rishi enjoyed Travis's antics. "Religion's similar to a mode of ground transport to travel to the airport."

"Religions are just the means?" said Travis.

"Yes, their purpose is to get you to the airport."

"The airport being God?" asked Travis.

"The airport being the gateway to God," said Rishi.

"The gateway being our soul?" asked Travis.

"Yes. Now, whichever mode of transport you use, once you reach the airport you don't need it anymore."

"Of course," said Travis.

"In fact," said Rishi, "at the check-in gate, they don't ask how you arrived. Once you're there and have the right papers, you board the plane and take off."

"The soul doesn't care how you got to it."

"Exactly," said Rishi, "If you refuse to step out because you love your Rolls-Royce, you'll never board the plane. To take the flight you must leave behind your ground transportation."

"Lost me there…," said Travis.

"Remember when we talked about the crutches?"

"Need to ditch the crutches to fully walk?" said Travis.

"Yes, this is the very same point. Religion is a tool that helps you, but if you really want to experience spirituality then at the appropriate time you have to leave religion behind."

"Religion is just a tool, just the means," said Travis. "Different than what I've heard all my life, but I'll buy it."

"Let me push you further," said Rishi.

Travis sat back up straight. He readied himself for what he knew would be another mind-twisting statement.

Rishi smiled his all-knowing smile. "Our notion of God, the name with which we recognize God…."

Travis listened with eyes wide open.

"Krishun, Christ, Allah, whatever else we call God, is only valid for our mind." Rishi raised his voice, "It has no bearing on our spirit!" Rishi swiftly sliced the air with his hands.

Travis felt a large meteor had hit him. The sonic boom ringing in his ears. Not because he thought it was a profound declaration but because he was having trouble reconciling what it meant. He felt his mind drowning. "Come again!"

"God is a concept — only for the purposes of our mind!"

"Are you saying God exists only in our mind?" said Travis.

"I knew you'd ask that," said Rishi tapping the side table with his fingers. "I'm not saying God only exists in our mind. I'm saying whatever we think about God, whatever we know about God, resides in our mind. If the mind's gone, so is our understanding, knowledge, and the very concept of God."

Travis nodded tentatively.

"The notion of God is a limited tool in your arsenal," said Rishi, "when you meditate and your mind is completely quiet, you must divorce from the thought of God itself."

Travis smiled, amazed at Rishi's explanations.

Then like a magician readying the audience for his big act, Rishi said, "And, here's the kicker…."

"What?" said Travis, excited as a kid at a magic show.

"To truly experience God, you must give up God." Rishi smiled as the magician who had successfully executed his act. He offered no further explanation to see how Travis responds.

Travis thought about it deeply. "I get it," he said, beaming he had unraveled the magician's trick. "Give up the notion of God in your mind, so it doesn't prevent you from experiencing the real God through your soul!"

Travis was proud, but not half as proud as Rishi,

To truly experience God, you must give up God.

who looked at Travis in true adoration. "Bravo!" said Rishi as he clapped. Pointing to Travis he said, "You have it!"

Travis remained sitting, still in a slight daze.

Mimicking the voice of an elderly statesman, Travis said, "Pretty philosophical!"

Rishi snickered. "Pretty philosophical," he said trying to copy Travis, but his accent betrayed him.

They both laughed. The realization was dawning on both of them how profound their discussion was.

"Our mind lacks the capability and comprehension to understand God in His full and true magnificence," said Rishi. "Therefore, we must put aside our limited and most likely faulty view of God in our minds, and experience the infinite and true view of God through our souls!"

Rishi pressed his palms together, "I pray to God daily, but when I meditate I have to leave at the door every notion of him, so I'm able to travel within and experience the true Him through my soul. The God in my mind is the Rolls Royce of ground transportation. As beautiful as it is, if I don't give it up I'll be stuck on Earth. To travel through the Universe, I need to experience the real infinite God associated with my soul, that formless, nameless, fathomless phenomenon. We all must discard our limited notion of God in our mind, so we can experience the infinite through our soul."

"Love you, buddy!" said Travis as he smiled from ear to ear. "You make complex philosophy simple!"

"Thanks," said Rishi with a gentle smile. He was immersed in his own words. "I'm really thankful," said Rishi, "to the Universe for this wisdom, and for the words to share it."

"I'm so thankful to benefit from it," said Travis. He stood up and walked with his right hand extended toward Rishi. Rishi got up, shook his hand, and they hugged. It was to thank each other for their presence. Their minds peaceful and yet dizzy, the embrace was reaffirming to their beings.

As they stepped back and sat down, Travis said, "I can't wait to experience the soul."

"Me too," said Rishi. "Spirituality is the Universe's most profound gift. But we can't receive the gift unless we overcome our biggest stumbling block — our own mind. Learning to manage the mind and breaking free of its hold is our most important job on Earth. Then nature and the Universe will do the rest."

Travis stomped. "Let's kick butt on our mind."

Rishi felt a little growl in his stomach. He looked at his watch. It was 11:30. "How we doing on time?" Rishi asked. "I love this discussion, I could go on all day, what about you?"

"I have a team meeting at 2:00 PM... I love this discussion too. I loved what you've shared about spirituality, truly mind-boggling. But to make progress I need to learn how to manage the mind... I'll push back my team meeting."

"Are you sure?" asked Rishi.

"We have a lot of work...," said Travis. "I'll dedicate tomorrow to it, and ask my team to make progress today without me."

"Thank you for your time," said Rishi.

"No, thank you, for your time!" Travis did a salute.

Rishi smiled. "Shall we order some lunch, or would you like to go to the restaurants downstairs?"

"Please order in, gives us more time to talk," said Travis.

"Okay." Rishi fetched the room service menu and gave it to Travis. Travis picked chicken quesadillas. Rishi decided on eggplant parmigiana. "Drink? Desert?" asked Rishi.

"Iced tea. No Desert, thanks," said Travis.

Rishi dialed room service and ordered the food. Travis answered his emails and texts. As Rishi walked back, he saw Travis frantically typing away with a frown. Once he was done, Rishi asked, "Everything okay?"

"Yeah, one of the team members doesn't get it, frustrating!" said Travis, "But I'll take care of it."

"The whole team is at the rented house?" asked Rishi.

"Yeah. Two of my team members live in Austin, so it was a good way to bring the whole team together. Helps us makes quick changes to the presentations and the demos as we get feedback from the investor meetings."

"Investor conference is all next week?" asked Rishi.

"Starts Tuesday. Venture capital firms from across the country are coming. We have three meetings set up, and I need to add many more as I network with the other investors."

Be religious to calm your mind, but never forget, religion is the means, not the end.

Religion is for your mind, your soul is unaffected by your religion.

Chapter 12: Transform Your Thoughts

Travis asked, "So how do I manage my mind, with all that's going on? How do I stay sane?"

Rishi swirled his finger. "The spiritual path is a great way to manage our minds. Do you remember the three steps?"

"Uh...."

Spiritual Path

*"Quiet your hungry mind,
let your happy soul shine!"*

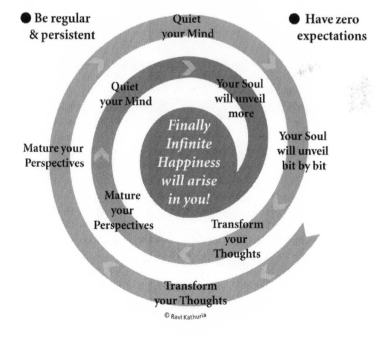

● Be regular & persistent

Quiet your Mind

● Have zero expectations

Quiet your Mind

Your Soul will unveil more

Finally Infinite Happiness will arise in you!

Mature your Perspectives

Your Soul will unveil bit by bit

Mature your Perspectives

Transform your Thoughts

Transform your Thoughts

© Ravi Kathuria

Rishi said, "Transform your thoughts, mature your perspectives, and quiet your mind. If we transform our thoughts, it can change our lives right away."

"That's great," said Travis smiling at Rishi's salesmanship.

"Before we transform our thoughts, it's important to understand the impact of our thinking," said Rishi. "Let me share a story. In ancient India, two boys wanted to become disciples of a great sage. The sage decided to test them. He gave both a dove and said, 'Go to a place where no one's watching or aware of your actions, and kill the dove.'"

"Okay," said Travis.

"The first boy found a cave, made sure no was watching, killed the dove, and came back excitedly. The sage looked at the dead bird, and asked him to wait."

Travis smirked.

"After several hours, the second boy came back with the dove alive. The sage asked why he had failed. He replied, 'I was about to kill the bird when I realized the bird was watching me. But, I justified it by saying the bird was the object of the test so maybe it doesn't count. Next, I realized God was watching. But, I justified it by saying I haven't seen God so maybe He doesn't count. Finally, I was ready to kill the bird, but I realized —'"

"What?" said Travis.

"The boy said, 'Oh, respected guru — I was watching. And no matter, how hard I tried, I was always aware. Even if I set up a rock to fall on the bird, and stepped away, I was still aware." A mild vibration went up Rishi's back. "The sage made the second boy his disciple and sent the first boy away."

Travis said, "Can't hide from our own mind."

"That's a really important point," said Rishi. "We must choose our thoughts carefully as they leave impressions on our mind. Negative thoughts leave negative impressions, making us cynical, while positive thoughts leave positive impressions making us optimistic."

> *You cannot cheat your mind! It sees and registers everything.*

"Be positive, I've read that so many times," said Travis.

"A single thought is harmless," said Rishi, "but an unending series of similar thoughts and resulting actions take on huge proportions."

"Water," said Travis, "when it flows continuously it'll even cut through rock, like the Grand Canyon."

"Great example. The power of repetition!" said Rishi. "We first generate the impressions, and then the impressions define us. The stronger the impressions, the more we're drawn to them."

> *A constant series of similar thoughts and actions can take on huge proportions.*

Travis rolled his fingers. "Feeds on itself."

"Have you heard the quote," said Rishi, "'Watch your thoughts for they become words, watch words they become actions, actions become habits, habits become your character, and, your character becomes your destiny!'"

"Powerful!" said Travis. "What we think we become."

"Every action, thought, and feeling is recorded in our subconscious mind," said Rishi. "We must respect this phenomenon. Our past impressions and anxieties molds our personalities." Rishi drew his hands apart. "We have to decompress years of impressions to free ourselves."

"Then our mind won't behave like a bull in a china shop?"

"Hopefully. Can't promise that in your case," joked Rishi.

Travis waved his finger, indicating he will get back.

Rishi smiled. "We must choose the right thoughts."

"Okay, I'll bite, which are the right thoughts?" said Travis.

"Ah." Rishi held up his index finger. "Right thoughts aren't about morality. It's about choosing the thoughts that make us peaceful. Do our thoughts make us calmer or more disturbed?"

"Good answer." Travis gave a firm nod.

Rishi smiled. "Thank you, your Honor."

"Okay, so which thoughts make us more disturbed?" asked Travis. "How should we transform our thoughts?"

"Let's start with the first point. We generate a lot of thoughts in fantasizing and worrying about our future. When we think about the future excessively we disturb our peace."

"An appointment with the future may cause disappointment," rhymed Travis as he bobbed.

"Good one," said Rishi. "When I was a manager, I couldn't wait to be a director. Then, I wanted to be a VP. Now, I can't wait to be a CEO. I'm always waiting for an outcome in the future. Life's never about the destination because when we get to the destination, we want a new destination."

"Love the journey," said Travis. "Future never comes."

"Yes, therefore, we should direct our thoughts toward the present. To become peaceful, we should spend less than ten percent of our thoughts on the future."

"You're right. I spend a majority of my thought on the future and not the present," said Travis. "Good advice."

"That's great advice!" Rishi playfully patted himself.

"We think about the future so we can control our destiny," said Travis.

"That's delusional," said Rishi.

"No, it's common sense," said Travis.

"We'll die trying, but destiny will never be in our control," said Rishi.

"Umm... not sure about that...," said Travis.

"We can't control our destiny, we can only control our effort and attitude," said Rishi. "We need to do our best and be prepared for destiny to take its course."

> *Spend less than ten percent of your thoughts on the future, and ninety percent on the present.*

> *We cannot control the outcome, we can only control our effort and attitude.*

Travis leaned forward. "Can you explain?"

"Sure, any outcome is dependent on several factors, many of them out of our control. Anyone who says they can control their destiny is misguided and isn't acknowledging the behind-the-scenes factors that contribute to the outcome happening. Staying focused on your effort and only taking ownership of your effort, keeps you humble and hungry."

"Like the Houston Rockets motto," said Travis.

"Yes. When you take ownership by claiming you can produce an outcome, you plant the seeds of arrogance and ego. You open yourself up for potential disappointment."

"I think I need an example," said Travis.

"Ok. A basketball team can never guarantee a win."

"Of course, they can, if they play hard," said Travis.

"No, they can't. Depends on how the other team plays. There are several other factors too, the most important, player injuries on both teams," said Rishi.

"Okay, yeah," said Travis.

"No team can ever say they're going to win a game. All they can say is we're going to play like we have never played before. We'll outdo all our previous performances."

"Focus on the effort, not on the outcome," said Travis.

"Yes, then, when they're behind they won't be dejected, and when ahead they won't become complacent. They'll play their best regardless of the score." Rishi sliced the air.

> *To find peace in life, focus on the effort not on the outcome.*

"It's called poise, playing with poise," said Travis.

Rishi smiled. "Yes, it is. I remember when the Rockets won the championships, they were playing the New York Knicks. When the Knicks were down, Patrick Ewing, their star player would throw a fit, when they were up, he'd strut around. On the Rockets side, Hakeem Olajuwon always kept his calm. Up or down, the Rockets would just play their game."

"Man, you're an oldie!" Travis rolled his eyes in jest.

"Excuse me!"

"Yeah man, those names are from a hundred years ago…"

"No, they're not." Rishi protested by playfully stomping his right foot. "It's a big deal you know, it was a huge win for the Rockets. Anyways, the top athletes are so well-focused on doing their part regardless of the situation. Imagine the intense pressure they must feel. We need to learn from them. You remember, at the Houston Super Bowl, Tom Brady and the Patriots delivered the biggest comeback in football history."

"Shocking!" Travis's face lit up. "Incredible game!"

"I've great respect for Steph Curry," said Rishi. "He's phenomenal! I'm impressed with how he's become the best three-point shooter, even though he was completely disregarded during his school years."

"Reinvented basketball!" said Travis. "They said he wasn't cut out for it! He showed them. Man, he's unnnnbelievable. Doesn't change the fact you're an oldie." Travis chuckled.

"Wanna play a game of racquetball Mr. I-am-youthful?" Rishi shook his torso, his competitive spirit on full display.

Both laughed.

"Now, what was I talking about...," said Rishi, "yes, the effort's the only thing under our control, the outcome's not."

"Okay, I agree... but, aren't outcomes good motivators?"

"Using outcomes as motivators is like using steroids to build muscles. Works in the short term but hurts you in the long term. Do you have a goal to be a $1 billion company?"

"Better believe it," said Travis.

"Bet that's a super strong motivator."

"Drives you, man, really motivates you."

"What happens during those weeks and months, when you feel that outcome is less likely, or you feel it's drifting away."

"It's horrible." Travis clamped his jaw and clenched his fist.

Rishi watched Travis's reaction. "The outcome has such a strong hold on you, just thinking about not achieving it is causing this visceral reaction."

Becoming conscious of himself, Travis eased up.

Rishi said, "I bet the times you find the goal is moving away are highly demotivating and frustrating?"

"Frustrating beyond imagination," said Travis.

"Obsessing about outcomes will always cause an emotional roller coaster. It'll drive you crazy, and exhaust you mentally."

> *Obsessing about outcomes will exhaust you mentally.*

"Exactly what's happening to me, but if I don't have the fire for achieving the outcome won't my effort be lackluster?"

"Not focusing on the outcome doesn't mean you ease up," said Rishi. "Put all your energy into your effort. Let that be the motivator. The fire for the outcome, as you called it, will only end up burning you. Focus on your effort. It's less emotionally draining. When I want to lose weight, I don't weigh myself."

"Why?" asked Travis.

"My weight's the outcome. The other outcome I don't want to think about is how I'll look when I'll be thin."

"Isn't goal visualization good?" asked Travis.

"It can be counter-productive," said Rishi. "When you're down 28 points at half-time during the Super Bowl, victory visualization is meaningless in motivating you."

"Will only visualize defeat at that point," said Travis.

"Exactly. Any hope will be drowned by despair. Your mind won't accept it. Visualizing the goal traps the mind in the outcome, and swings it violently between hope and despair. So, instead of measuring weight, I measure how many steps I walk and how many calories I take in every day. That's all I watch."

"That's interesting," said Travis.

"It's liberating, I don't have to worry if I'm losing weight or not. The pressure is off. Previously, I used to weigh myself, and then some days the news is good and some it's not. Now, I weigh myself once a month, not every day. When you focus on the effort, there's less emotional drama. You just say I need to walk more so I can get my quota done. That's your only focus. Simple."

"I'll be darned," said Travis.

"What do you mean?" said Rishi.

"You're making sense, Master Yoda." Travis bobbed, referring to the character from the Star Wars movies.

"Why're you surprised, Obi-Wan?" said Rishi playfully.

Travis smiled. "If I stop worrying about the outcome... I might... I could be free."

"Bingo." Rishi jabbed his finger in the air.

"Can I really do it?" asked Travis.

"We all can. This is a powerful transformation in our thinking that can relieve us and make us more peaceful."

"Kinda like the saying, why worry about the things you can control because you can control them, and why worry about the things you can't control because you can't control them."

"Mine has a deeper philosophical point," said Rishi.

"Of course, Mr. Professor," said Travis as he rolled his hand as a show of playful respect.

Rishi smiled and said in a serious tone, "Enjoy your effort since the outcomes may not happen the way you want, and even if they do you'll chase new outcomes."

"Let me see... how you said it, you can control your effort, not your outcome," said Travis. Then he raised his hand, "I can do better — love your effort not your outcome."

"You're a good student," said Rishi.

"I'm the best!" Travis thumped his chest.

Travis's energy and spontaneity always created a positive vibe for Rishi.

Love your effort not the outcome.

"That's the second point in transforming our thoughts — love your effort not your outcome," said Rishi.

"Do real people derive happiness from the effort and ignore the outcome," asked Travis. "Does that happen? Really?"

"It does. Teachers derive joy from teaching, even though they don't witness the success their kids achieve. True painters paint for inner satisfaction and not for external appreciation."

"Well… okay," said Travis. He wanted examples that are more robust but did not verbalize his thought.

"I'd tell Priya, study not because you want a good grade but because you enjoy it," said Rishi. "When I ask college students what they want in life, do you know what they say?"

"Money?" replied Travis with a grin.

"Yes. Rarely, does one say they want to do work that'll make them truly happy and content. In today's society, we celebrate the outcome, not the effort. It's making us shallower, ultimately causing discontent. There's great joy in loving our work and doing effort for the sake of effort. Those who enjoy their effort without regard to the outcomes are blessed."

Travis hesitated. "Does that… should I give up my goals?"

"No, never," said Rishi. "My point is your goals are not as sacrosanct as you might've thought. Work toward your goals, by all means, and with all your heart, yet make sure those goals exist for you and you don't exist for those goals."

"Not sure what that means," said Travis.

"Don't let your goals become a chronic obsession, don't fall in love with them. Use them as a roadmap, as opposed to being the be all and end all. And, choose goals carefully."

"How?" asked Travis.

"Do not make losing weight a goal. It's an outcome."

"Ah, make goals about the effort, eat healthy, exercise."

"Yes," said Rishi, "and at Travisto too, but make sure you include goals that focus on the development and effort as well, in addition to outcomes such as revenues and growth."

"Measure both effort and outcome," said Travis. "This is good. I'll go back and revisit Travisto's goals."

"Do that. If you transform your thoughts toward your efforts, you'll experience a new freedom, because outcomes won't suffocate you. Your anxiety and stress will go down. You will find greater joy and become more peaceful. And amazingly, you'll become more successful. It's a paradox, the less you think about outcomes, the more you'll achieve them."

"Don't ignore outcomes, but don't obsess about them." Travis exhaled almost as if he was breathing out his stress.

Rishi did a thumbs up and then held up three fingers. "I want to talk about the third point under transforming our thoughts. It has a sweeping effect on our attitude and prepares our mind for quietude."

"Okay," said Travis. "What's that?"

"Moderation. It's a powerful technique." Rishi shook his head. "If I'd moderated, my life would've been much better. Whenever I've screwed up, it's because I've overindulged."

"How?" asked Travis.

"You've been to our house?" asked Rishi. He lived in the fast-growing, lush, family friendly suburb of Sugar Land.

"Yup, lovely house on the water," said Travis.

"I wanted a bigger, more beautiful house," said Rishi.

"Why, it was just the three of you?"

"Well, my friends had nicer homes. We had lived in ours for ten years. I over-extended buying the new house, wish we'd stayed put. Suchi did her best to dissuade me."

"Why didn't you listen to her, man?"

"Wish I had." Rishi looked wistful. "I'd look online at homes for sale, never realized when it took such a strong hold. I wanted a nice home theater, bigger garage, nicer lake view. I wanted to feel good at parties, talking about where we lived."

"Was it your addiction?" asked Travis.

"Certainly became one. I couldn't stop myself, even though we didn't need it. If Suchi discouraged me, I was ready to fight. If my realtor said something, I was ready to fire her even if she was just trying to help me. Due to my ego, I lost my objectivity."

"That's not good," said Travis.

"I know," said Rishi. "I enjoy the new house very much, but I've lost sleep worrying about paying for it. Now that I look back, I didn't need to buy a six thousand square feet home."

Travis widened his eyes. "That's huge!"

"It was fine when I had a job, but when I lost it —"

"You did?"

"I didn't have a job for eighteen months," said Rishi.

"That's long."

"No kidding, that beautiful house became such a burden. A less expensive house wouldn't have caused so much stress."

"You didn't know you'd lose your job," said Travis.

"No, I didn't —"

"Why didn't you sell it off?" asked Travis.

"The Oil & Gas industry took jobs away, and it also killed the real estate market. Didn't want to take a big loss."

"Double whammy!" Travis punched his fist into his palm.

Rishi shook his head. "Whenever I've forgotten to moderate I've ended up in trouble. I've chased returns in stocks, fantasized about the money and then burnt myself. I've made mistakes and then my ego hasn't allowed me to accept those mistakes. My advice, invest in stocks, but moderate your fantasy about the profits you'll make."

"I don't get that," said Travis.

"Well, when you become greedy, you may have healthy profits but you hold out for more and end up losing it all," said Rishi. "There's a saying among stock investors, 'Pigs get slaughtered.' I've learned it the hard way."

"Uh, uh," said Travis. "Many of the technology stocks have gone up for years. Selling those stocks would be stupid."

"If your decisions are based on fundamental and technical analysis, and sound risk management, you're good. In my case, it was wishful thinking, based on ego, hope, and prayer."

Travis nodded. "That would be a problem."

"Moderation is not my concept," said Rishi, "It's a law of nature. Without salt and sugar, food isn't tasty, and your body needs them to function well. But overconsumption can create serious health issues. Same with the material world — take only the right amount to have a happy life. Know when it's too little and when it's too much."

"How do I know when it's enough?" asked Travis.

"Don't let anything have a strong hold on you, whether it's work, relationships, emotions, possessions, whatever else."

Travis digested the point. "Travisto has a big hold on me."

"I know. Remember, we talked about passion versus obsession. Have a passion for Travisto, not obsession."

"How do I tell when it's an obsession?" asked Travis.

"Obsession will induce fear, anxiety, irritability, and mood swings. Passion will give you positivity and dedication. Make sure Travisto exists for you, not the other way around."

"What do you mean?" asked Travis.

"Don't let your happiness be hostage to the company. Travisto is only one aspect of your life. A very important aspect, I'll give you that, but it's only one aspect. Work really hard on Travisto, but if for some reason it doesn't succeed, walk away without losing your confidence or motivation, reapply yourself to another opportunity."

"Yessss… but I can't let it fail —" said Travis.

"See, that's the trap."

"What?" Travis raised his brow.

"Say, I don't want it to fail, rather than I can't let it fail," said Rishi. "By saying I can't, you're taking ownership. Don't be in bondage. When you say, I don't want it to fail, you're saying I'm going to do everything I can, but I'm still the master. Your life is much more important, much bigger than one company."

"I've thought about that," said Travis. "When I was in Houston, I had time to do stuff. Travisto has sucked my entire life since I started it."

"Then moderate how much hold Travisto has on you. You might actually generate more success."

Travis fidgeted slightly. Rishi let the point sink in.

Rishi said, "If we step away from our addictions it'll provide instant relief from our burdens, reduce our worries, make our lives better, and uplift us towards peace." A message intended as much for Travis as himself.

There was a knock. "Room service."

Rishi opened the door. "Come on in." As the server set up lunch on the round mahogany table by the bar, Travis stepped toward the window and responded to emails on his phone. Rishi thanked the server as he left. Travis walked to the table with a pensive look but he smiled before Rishi could notice.

"How's the quesadilla?" asked Rishi.

"Pretty good, but this salsa is quite hot!" said Travis.

"I like spicy, let me try some." Rishi spooned himself some of the salsa. "Woo ooh, that's spicy — even for me."

Travis wiped his eyes. "Not having any more of that."

Rishi laughed. "It should come with a warning."

"Did say habanero," said Travis.

"Lucky you didn't go in deep." Rishi smiled suggestively.

"What?"

"This world is like this habanero salsa," said Rishi. "If you aren't careful and dip too deep, it'll get really spicy."

"Can find an analogy in anything, can't you?"

"Of course, I can," said Rishi smiling.

Rishi put his fork down. "Remember the fish lady story?"

"Yeah," said Travis.

"I'm caught up in stocks, you in Travisto. We need to train ourselves to sleep without our stinky fish. Moderation will help us gain freedom from our bubbles," said Rishi.

"Moderation's a lot harder than you make it sound. Just thinking about putting mental distance between Travisto and me is difficult. I mean, it's a complete mess right now."

"I know. It's not easy to tell the mind to let go. So many people fail to diet because willpower only works for so long."

"So, how should they do it?" asked Travis.

"The people who succeed don't diet," said Rishi.

"What do you mean?" said Travis.

"It's a lifestyle change," said Rishi. "They change their habits slowly. They don't cut off sweets completely. They moderate the quantity and frequency. After months and years, their outlook on desserts changes. They don't stop their mind cold turkey. They train themselves to get over desserts. They still enjoy desserts but the hold becomes lesser."

"So what's my lifestyle change?" asked Travis.·

"Ah, start with baby steps. Stop checking emails and messages all the time, especially in the evenings. I need to stop checking stock prices every hour. If we cut back on the stimuli, it'll allow us to create a buffer," said Rishi.

"That's not easy, things change constantly."

"Learn to take some time off. Try reducing the frenzy, that'll give you the upper hand. Then, you'll make better decisions for you and Travisto."

Travis did not respond.

They finished lunch. Rishi made a trip to the restroom. Travis went back to answering his texts and emails.

> *A glutton eats too much, an anorexic eats too little — both are wrong. Only moderation is healthy.*

When Rishi returned, Travis said, "We're like race car drivers, and our minds are like the engine. To win the race we need our minds, but if we push the engine beyond the operating range, we'll burn it."

"Nice analogy," said Rishi.

"Problem is I don't have the luxury of slowing down, I'll get run over," said Travis. "Even right now, I have a fire raging in my team. It's driving me crazy!"

"You realize, as long as you live, these fires won't go away."

"Isn't that the ugly truth," said Travis.

"Do you know how moderation helps? It reduces the quantity of thought," said Rishi.

"Interesting angle — reducing the quantity of thought."

"If you have fewer thoughts, you'll be more peaceful. That is basic and that is powerful," said Rishi. "If you're addicted to thinking about Travisto, you'll feel like a hamster in the wheel. Moderate the quantity of Travisto thoughts and see if it makes a difference. I'll bet you'll find easier and faster success."

Travis listened quietly.

Rishi gestured a car. "Your race car analogy —"

"Bring the mind within the operating range," said Travis.

"Yes. Thinking excessively will burn the engine or make it inefficient. Be in the range to maximize your productivity."

"Like a computer. If I run too many applications, it'll make everything run slower," said Travis.

"Now, why didn't I think about it?" said Rishi.

"You know why…." Travis eyed Rishi mischievously.

"No, I don't like just old analogies," said Rishi widening his eyes, "I can think of modern ones too."

Travis grinned. Rishi smiled too. Rishi said, "If you focus ninety percent of your thoughts on the present as opposed to the future, if you focus ninety percent of your thoughts on the effort as opposed to the outcome, and if you moderate your thoughts, you will feel freer, lighter and unshackled. This will boost your wellbeing, productivity, and creativity."

"You better be right," said Travis.

"Only way we'll know is if you try it," said Rishi.

"Okay," said Travis. "I'll give it a shot."

"Next, I want to talk about transforming our thoughts so we can be happier. Changing how we think can have such a big impact on our happiness."

Transform Your Thoughts

Live in the present, not in the future and not in the past.

Love your effort, not the outcome. Obsessing about outcomes will undermine your success.

Enjoy but moderate. Be a slave to nothing. The ability to engage at an arm's length without obsession and addiction is a powerful way to calm the mind.

If you live in the future and/or chase outcomes, you will live with anxiety and stress. If you love your effort, you will experience heavenly joys.

If you moderate your mental addictions, it will provide you refreshing freedom.

Chapter 13: Happiness Mindset

Rishi caressed his forehead. "We need to cultivate a mindset for happiness. If we're happier in the material world, it helps our spiritual progress. A troubled or disturbed mind hinders progress. I have three points to share. The first one is about expectations. We expect things to be perfect all the time."

"That's normal," said Travis.

"That's a mistake, it steals our happiness. I want my wife to always listen to me, I want my stocks to always go up, I want the traffic to disappear when I drive. I want my boss to give me a promotion on my timetable. We think, if only, life would behave according to my wishes, then I'd be perfectly happy."

"Life's not going to be perfect," said Travis.

"No, it's not, but, if we change our expectations, life, with all its problems, can be happier. Our expectations determine our level of happiness and the quality of our life."

"It's defeatist to have low expectations," said Travis.

Rishi shook his finger. "Not low expectations, right expectations. When you leave, expect to find traffic. Whether you're upset or not, you'll still arrive at the same time. So relax, listen to music, and reach in a good mood. Let life take its course. Don't expect a perfect life, expect ups and downs, be prepared to face the challenges and be ready to solve them with a smile. Don't be buried by the wave of life, ride it."

"Ride the wave with a smile." Travis swayed his hand.

"Yes. Religions advise us to selflessly help those who are suffering. When we help others it calms us, gives us relief, making us realize our problems are smaller."

Travis nodded.

"The second point is we should never complain. People with great attitude don't complain, they work on making the best of their life. So many people have the right attitude. Cancer ravaging their bodies, tornadoes destroying their homes, economy destroying their livelihood, nothing fazes them, they're the true heroes. They know how to accept the hard facts, let go of the past, and move forward. I'm in awe of them."

Travis listened.

"Complaining drains us, makes us weaker," said Rishi. "If you say, I'm not going to complain anymore, it'll make you feel better."

We cannot control the circumstance, we can only control our reaction.

"Sometimes it's hard not to complain."

"True," said Rishi, "many times life feels unfair, we begrudge life and even others' success. The problem is when we're thinking about what could've, should've been, we're not applying ourselves to improve our situation."

"Sometimes the situation is out of control," said Travis.

"I know, but we can still work on how we react, how we deal with situations. Our reaction is always under our control."

"We can't control the circumstance, we can only control our reaction," said Travis turning philosopher.

"That's right." Rishi did a thumbs up. "We wallow in self-pity, why's this happening to me. We have self-doubt, I'm not good, I'll never be successful, I'm not lucky, I'm not smart. All these thoughts rob us of our potential and our happiness."

"Some people are unlucky and incapable. Can't help it."

"We all have been dealt with different cards, someone else probably is smarter, luckier," said Rishi. "We can't change that, we must play the best game with the cards we have been dealt."

"My mother always said that," said Travis.

"She's right. Complaining steals our happiness and makes us miserable. If we have a positive attitude we'll have more success than we had coming our way," said Rishi.

"Makes sense."

"Stephen Hawking, the legendary physicist had a debilitating disease for fifty years, but he never complained," said Rishi. "A quote from him says, 'If one is physically disabled, one cannot afford to be psychologically disabled as well.'"

"Not everyone can be strong like that," said Travis. "But I get the point. A military friend told me you never want to come back from battle with bullets left in your pocket."

> *Never come back from a battle with bullets left in your pocket.*

Rishi beamed. "Love that! We may have different types of bullets, but, we must fire every bullet, that's all we can do. Unfortunately, our thinking is so ingrained we don't realize it. Consider an investor who's built a net worth of $25 Million."

Travis smiled. "Cool!"

"Then the stock market crashes and he's only left with $12 Million. How'd he feel?" asked Rishi.

"Horrible," said Travis.

"If I gave you $12 Million, how'd you feel?" asked Rishi.

"Ecstatic!" said Travis.

"Why?"

"It's a lot of money. My worries would be over —"

"Then why's the investor miserable, he has $12 Million?"

"Well…."

"His mind would torture him because he doesn't have the $13 Million," said Rishi. "Yet, he still has $12 Million, something that could be a source of heaven-ness for you."

Travis got up and walked up to the window. "Why is that? He has the money, yet he feels like a failure."

"You don't have an expectation of $25 Million, so $12 Million is a huge blessing. Being left with only $12 Million is a debilitating curse for the investor." Rishi touched his forehead. "Heaven and hell exist in our own minds."

"Well… if I lost $13 million I'd go crazy, I wouldn't sleep until I made it back." Travis sat down. "I understand right expectations, but how's striving for more a bad thing? Trying to regain what you've lost, how's that bad? I don't get that."

"Trying to regain the $13 million isn't bad by itself. It's bad if we don't enjoy what we have, and become miserable, focused on what we don't have or what we have lost. Striving for more, wanting to grow are healthy traits, but they're a curse if they stop us from enjoying what we have. We take life for granted, and miss out," said Rishi.

Travis listened.

> *Do not take life for granted. Have gratitude.*

"Our lives are a huge blessing," said Rishi, "yet we have little gratitude. You talked about rich kids, they have everything and yet they're always complaining. Caught like the hamster in the wheel, we don't relish life. You're frustrated because you're not achieving success fast enough, but if you ask my wannabe entrepreneur friends, they'll say they're envious of you. We all want a different life, more perfect than the one we have. If we have gratitude, it can be the foundation of our happiness mindset. If the Lord appeared, we wouldn't be able to ask for anything else because we have all the comforts."

Travis's eyes flickered. "I know what I'd ask."

Rishi lifted his head slightly.

Travis answered, "Money... Nathan." Travis's face contorted. "I'll ask God to give me back my son...."

"Travis...." Rishi struggled. "Travis...." Rishi looked away and then back at Travis. "Please don't hold up your life because of Nathan... please focus on what you have."

Travis looked down.

"Focus on Cindi. Focus on yourself. That's the reality now. If you ignore yourself, if you ignore your wife, you're not relishing the life you have now."

If you desire peace, focus your thoughts on what you have, not on what you do not have.

Travis flushed red.

"No one can bring Nathan back...," said Rishi as carefully as he could, "but that doesn't mean you should stop enjoying life, and punish yourself."

"I don't punish myself," said Travis in a stark voice.

"Are you working harder," said Rishi, "spending all the time at work, to avoid…."

Travis squirmed. His body stiff and face lifeless.

Rishi closed his eyes and took a few gentle breaths. "Let there be peace… let there be peace." He lightly gestured with both his palms in the air, as if he was caressing someone.

Travis eased a little.

"My daughter got married in India. I must choose to be happy even if I miss her like crazy. A choice I must make every day. Happiness is a difficult and yet absolutely necessary choice we must make even in the most horrible of circumstances."

Travis did not respond.

"Choosing to be happy is the third point," said Rishi, "it's the positive transformation we need in our thoughts and lives."

Happiness is a choice — we must make!

Travis tried to speak, but Rishi raised his hand gently. "You deserve to be happy. Your son died," said Rishi in a soft tone, "yet you must choose to be happy. And," said Rishi his voice rising, "you can't be lackadaisical. Choosing to be happy isn't something you do casually. Choosing to be happy is something you must do with full active effort."

"That's hard," murmured Travis shaking his head.

"I know," said Rishi. "Paralysis crippled Stephen Hawking, but instead of focusing on his body he focused on that fact he still had his super-intelligent brain. You must make the choice to be happy, for you and your wife's sake, and for your team."

Travis stayed silent.

"May I offer a suggestion?" asked Rishi.

"Go ahead," said Travis in a somber tone.

"Next time you see a boy who's Nathan's age, walk away."

"Because it'll torture me later?" said Travis.

"Yes. Your mind likes Nathan's memories, so definitely do that in a measured manner by looking at his pictures and videos, but don't do that by looking at other people's kids."

Travis thought about it. "So, I don't begrudge others."

"Yes. You begin to ask again, why you had to suffer, why Nathan. Save yourself that torture. Until you become stronger, be vigilant, protect your mind and walk away. Being aware of how such a situation affects you, will insulate you."

"I hear you," said Travis in pain, "but I don't know how to fill the void. I can't stop missing him." Travis's eyes moistened.

"There was a rich merchant in ancient India," said Rishi.

It took a moment for Travis to reorient himself. He realized Rishi was sharing another story. He wiped his eyes.

"He was afraid of thieves, so he put all his wealth, which was primarily in gold coins, in a pot and buried the pot under one of the trees in the backyard. Three years later, wanting to check on the pot, he dug up the area to find the pot was gone."

"Oh, no," said Travis.

"He'd been robbed. He couldn't eat or sleep. His health suffered. Concerned, his wife asked a sage to counsel him."

"What did the sage, say, don't be addicted to the gold?" teased Travis, sniffling, as a smile broke on his face.

Rishi smiled. "Mr. Smarty Pants! No, the sage said, take a pot, fill it with wooden coins, and bury it in the same place."

"Why? Sounds silly," said Travis.

"The merchant asked the same. The sage said just do it. So, the merchant did. Three months later the sage came back to check on the merchant. He had recuperated and was healthy."

"How?" said Travis.

"The merchant asked the sage, 'Why am I feeling better?'"

"What did the sage say?"

"The sage told the merchant, when he replaced the pot, even though the conscious mind realized it was full of wooden coins, his subconscious began to let go and relax. The new pot allowed the mind to break free of the vicious cycle of despair."

"Umm...."

"The merchant shared, 'But, oh sage, in a way I still feel I have the gold. Even though it's gone, when I sleep, some part of me is at peace having the pot there.' The sage smiled and left."

"Sounds like the sage was a psychiatrist," said Travis.

"We must understand how the mind works, to save ourselves from the misery the mind causes." Rishi looked into Travis's eyes. "Fill your void, Travis."

Travis did not respond.

Rishi said in a soothing tone, "Travis, you have many choices. You could have another child or adopt."

"Yeah... we don't want to do any of those," said Travis.

"Give love another chance. You have love inside you. The love of a father. Another child could give you happiness. You're not replacing Nathan or betraying his memory. Please give yourself the permission to be happy again."

Not getting a reaction from Travis, Rishi paused. "Okay, this may sound silly."

"Silly is fine." Travis tapped his thumb slightly.

"Get a giant teddy bear and place it in Nathan's room. Hug the bear every day," said Rishi.

Rishi waited for a reaction.

"We put a life-size picture of Nathan in his room."

Rishi grimaced. "Yeah, I'm not sure if that's the best idea. It'll continue to trouble your conscious mind, tug at it every time you look at the picture. It'd be similar to the merchant putting gold-plated coins in his room. That won't provide peace. We want to calm the conscious mind and then go to work on the subconscious mind for full relief. A bear won't directly bring up memories and might provide comfort."

Travis squinted. "Okay...."

"The first few days hugging the bear may be very emotional, similar to when the wound bursts. But the emotions will subside, and in a year the bear will go back to being a bear."

Travis closed his eyes. He imagined the bear and hugging it. It shook him a little, but it also had a comforting feeling to it.

Travis opened his eyes. "Mom's been telling me to have another child, but I've resisted. Cindi too would like to have a baby... I'll... think about it. But I'll definitely buy the bear."

"Please do." Rishi walked up to Travis, squeezed his shoulder and patted him. Then he walked back and sat down.

"I really liked your points for transforming thoughts," said Travis. "It has helped me. I'll transform how I think. And, I'll cultivate a happiness mindset. I do need to be happier... actually, I'm feeling a little happier already... I feel better."

"Wonderful! You deserve to be happier. We all do. Have the right expectations, never complain, and make the conscious choice to be happy every day. Then you'll feel happier and become more peaceful."

"I will." Travis nodded.

"As we go through the spiritual path, you'll see how it makes life better for us here in the material world and prepares us for spirituality. It's time to talk about upgrading our perspectives on life and this world. It'll give us new maturity."

**Transform
Your Thoughts**

↑

Live in the present,
not in the future and not
in the past.

Love your effort,
not the outcome.
Obsessing about
outcomes will undermine
your success.

Enjoy but moderate.
Be a slave to nothing. The
ability to engage at an
arm's length without
obsession and addiction
is a powerful way to calm
the mind.

Be happy now. Do not
complain about life,
instead focus on making
life better.

Be happy now. Have the
right expectations. Relish
what you have, do not
dwell on what you don't
have.

Make the choice to be
"happy" every day, even
during difficult times.

Strive for more, but do not be a slave to expectations.

Do not complain, do not begrudge. Fix or accept things. Always keep smiling.

Happiness is a choice. You have the power to decide if you want to be happy.

Be happier now!

Chapter 14: Mature Your Perspectives

Rishi touched his forehead. "It's difficult for our minds to calm down until we mature our perspectives. We must really understand how this world works, that's how we'll mature."

"Does maturity come with age?" asked Travis.

"Yes and no. Age sometimes leads to maturity."

"I must be the kind that matured young." Travis grinned.

"Of course." Rishi smiled. "I have three points to share. The first is our worldly bubble is fragile." He swept his hand around the room. "We think everything in life is guaranteed. When we're happy, having a blast, we don't see any problem."

Travis nodded slightly.

"But, sooner or later, our bubble bursts," said Rishi. "Life is full of ups and downs. When we're lost in a stupor, thinking we're in control, that's when life can hit us the hardest, reminding us things can change drastically without warning."

Travis was silent.

Rishi looked caringly at Travis. "Because we don't have the right perspective, we allow catastrophic events to overwhelm us and destroy our lives. The executive who works all the time suddenly loses his or her job, or worse, or is demoted. Such an executive is hit so hard, it seems like an existential crisis."

Travis grimaced. "My Dad's best friend worked for the same oil & gas company for 33 years and was laid off. That was his entire working life," said Travis. "He was devastated, took him a long time to recover."

"Life shocks us again and again," said Rishi. "Many years ago, a family friend's investments were wiped out in the stock market. He became bedridden and lost his will to live."

"I've seen people get badly hurt in love," said Travis. "One of my wife's friends nearly killed herself. We had no idea she was so heartbroken. But not everyone kills themselves."

"True, you don't have to kill yourself," said Rishi, "but it still gets pretty horrible. I've gone through my absolute hell."

"What happened?"

Rishi looked away. "If we remember our life's situations are fragile, then we're living with our eyes open, not flying blind."

"Isn't that living in fear?" said Travis.

"Not at all. Car accidents are a reality. Doesn't mean we stop driving, but, we should never forget accidents do happen. That's a reminder to not drive recklessly," said Rishi.

"I get it," said Travis. "In Las Vegas, the odds are always with the house. I tell my team don't delude yourself into thinking you're lucky and play without limits, you could lose your shirt. Delusion is injurious to health," joked Travis.

If we are not careful, we can lose our most precious asset — our inner peace!

"Consider this world as a supersized Las Vegas," said Rishi. "We can have a lot of ups and downs. If we live unaware, we're living recklessly. We don't even realize it — it's an epidemic!"

"Is it that bad? Really?" Travis had a doubtful look.

"More than you can imagine. Look at the amount of discontent we all experience in our lives. So many people go through depression because they feel life's failed them. And, then there's so many who suffer extreme stress and anxiety."

"Can't argue with that," said Travis.

"Okay, our worldly bubble is fragile, was the first point. The second point is nothing in this world is permanent. Everything we're concerned about, everything we love and hate, it's transient. In a hundred years it'll be all different."

Travis tapped his thumb. "None of us will be here then."

"Then why does it have such a hold?" said Rishi. "We're the only species who understands death is certain. Yet, we act as if we'll live forever. Our lives are temporary, like sand castles on the beach waiting to be dissolved by the tide."

"Don't wanna think about it, it's a downer."

Rishi smiled. "Actually, it's a liberator, gives us ultimate freedom. Wealth, family, friends, career, everything's transient. Once we accept it, we'll develop the right perspective and not take life too seriously. It'll free us from our fears and make us stronger. Make us like steel."

> *Nothing in the material world is permanent — nothing!*

"Well…." Travis pushed a pillow aside.

"Steve Jobs, the co-founder of Apple, had a great quote," said Rishi, "'Remembering you are going to die is the best way to avoid the trap of thinking you have something to lose.'" Rishi paused. "We have nothing to lose. Nothing on Earth is ours. We're tourists passing through."

"We do hang around for a long time," said Travis. "And, we leave our legacy behind."

"That's true. I'm not saying disregard life completely, I'm saying take it less seriously." Rishi took a deep breath. "There's something I've never shared with anyone...."

Unsure, Travis eyed Rishi with no reaction.

"When I was eighteen or nineteen... I used to think about killing myself by jumping from the terrace of our building."

"You're kidding me!" Travis lurched forward.

"Nope." Rishi shook his head.

"Why, why would you think something like that?"

"Pressure of doing well in exams," said Rishi.

"Pressure from parents?"

"No, self-pressure." Rishi looked down.

"That's terrible! How could you think like that?"

"Studies was my world. I didn't have any other interests. I needed to do well, and put a lot of pressure on myself."

"That was your bubble," said Travis.

"Yes, unfortunately," said Rishi. "I was a good student, but inside, I was dealing with nonsense. Exam pressure would give me this harrowing feeling —"

"No reason to jump off!" said Travis.

"Oh, agree completely, but then, in that situation, it was just overwhelming. The point is as horrible as it was... today, I can barely remember it. Can't even remember my grades. What was so compelling then seems like an illusion now."

Travis could not relate. Grades never mattered to him.

Rishi said, "I graduated with honors, yet, for many years I'd get nightmares I hadn't prepared enough."

"It had that strong a hold on you?" said Travis.

Rishi sighed. "In my early jobs, I used to be so worried about the politics, how my bosses were playing games —"

"Ugh, corporate America," said Travis.

"I used to be so stressed," said Rishi. "Suchi would ask me to take it easy, but I couldn't. Now, I can barely remember the names of my bosses, let alone my problems. At that time what seemed so real is a faint memory now."

"Can't argue that," said Travis. "I hated my three years in corporate America, now it does seem distant."

"I feel like a complete fool now," said Rishi. "Those situations have disappeared. I went through hell for nothing."

"Not true," said Travis, "You accomplished stuff."

Rishi unfurled his palm to gesture things disappearing. "My point is, nothing has stayed steady. Not even me. I can't find my younger self. I look in the mirror and wonder who's the guy I'm looking at. I ask him, 'Hey, who are you? How did you get in?'" Rishi widened his eyes and pushed his face forward as if he was looking in a mirror.

The tide of time will wash away our sand castles of physical body, relationships, work, assets, reputation and even our very identities! Why then are we so obsessed with the material world?

Travis smiled. "You're funny."

"I refuse Facebook requests from my high-school friends," said Rishi.

"Why?" said Travis, finding it difficult to relate.

"They look old in their pictures. My memory of them is much younger. I want to hang on to that. They've changed — I've changed."

"That's life," said Travis.

"Indeed it is. And, that is my point. The whole material world is transient. What seems so real now, so overwhelming now, will absolutely fade away with time. We need to remember that always, and not get bent out of shape in difficult times, or go overboard in good times."

"This too shall pass," said Travis.

Rishi wondered if Travis was referring to his situation or just reciting the common saying. "Travis, this point is critical in maturing our perspective. If we appreciate all of our life incidents are transient, then we won't take them too seriously, we won't be beaten or broken down. We'll engage with the material world, but not be shocked when things change."

Travis looked on painfully. He shook his head slowly. "I know where you're going with this. Someday, I'll get over... not get over... accept Nathan's death. I could've never been prepared for Nathan's... can't ever prepare for that."

Rishi nodded gently in acknowledgment. "In your case, it was sudden, in my case, it wasn't. Priya got married in India. I miss her so much, I don't get to talk to her much now. She's busy with her husband, in-laws, and her new business. The house is so empty... so lifeless without her."

"You're telling me."

"Suchi is consumed with her school work, I'm busy too but I'm really lonely. I miss our family times. I knew this was coming, yet I didn't develop other interests. The first few months after the wedding were just horrible."

Travis kept mum.

Rishi took a few breaths. "All of us are making the mistake of believing our lives will continue forever the way it is, we don't prepare ourselves for known and unknown changes."

Travis did not say anything.

His fingers interlocked, Rishi caressed the nail of his right thumb with his left thumb. "There are so many couples in their sixties, seventies, and eighties who need to be better prepared for one of them to pass away. They need to develop interests, occupations, and relationships beyond their spouse. Otherwise, life can be crushing for the first few months and years after their spouse passes away."

"Younger couples too," said Travis.

"Yes, them too." Rishi waved his hand. "Health, wealth, careers, relationships, are all fleeting."

"That's depressing." Travis contorted his face.

"It's ugly, but it's the truth," said Rishi. "Once we accept the truth, it gives us our toughness and the ultimate positive outlook on life. Takes the fear away. We can't change the laws of life, but we can change our perspective and be better prepared. It'll be difficult, but it'll be our greatest victory."

> *Everything you see, your possessions, your relationships, even your notion of GOD, is transient, subject to complete and sudden change.*

"This one is difficult." Travis sagged.

Rishi asked, "Do you remember the story where the king killed all the wild animals and built the palace on the island?"

"Yes." Travis thought about it. "So, we need to kill our fears and obsessions, and spirituality is the island palace."

"Very nice. If we progress toward spirituality, we'll insulate ourselves from the world. The ugliness won't affect us and we'll only see beauty all around us." Rishi smiled. "How about another depressing topic? It's my third point."

"Sure, why not," said Travis returning the smile.

"Actually wait, let me share something funny," said Rishi.

"Okay," Travis lifted himself.

"One day I had a thought that life is too short and I need to relish each day," said Rishi. "I love food, so I decided I need to have a great meal every day. Now, I don't know how to cook, Suchi does all the cooking. She is an excellent cook, but many days she'll just put together something quickly."

"Getting interesting," said Travis, smiling in anticipation.

"I wanted to tell Suchi, she needs to make a great meal every day. I knew if I just asked it wouldn't happen, so to be dramatic, while having dinner I told her, 'I am dying.'"

> *Tell your mind, I must relish today unconditionally and to its fullest!*

"You did not!" said Travis shaking his head.

"I did too. I thought she'll be shocked and concerned."

"Then?"

"Without even lifting her head, she said, 'We're all dying.'"

Travis burst out laughing.

Rishi laughed too. "Basically, she meant shut up and finish dinner. Priya, my very own daughter, didn't even look up and continued to eat ignoring the whole conversation. I learned an important lesson — eat dinner quietly without complaining."

"Serves you right!" said Travis wagging his finger.

"That's right," said Rishi caressing his forehead. "Oh, my."

"You mentioned another depressing thing," said Travis.

"Yes, my third point. We need to understand the nature of happiness," said Rishi.

"Excuse me, the nature of happiness?"

"Yes, we derive happiness from various sources. Possessions like houses, cars, clothes and bank balances. Pleasurable experiences and activities like dancing, playing sports, hiking. We enjoy a sense of community by going to a concert or watching sports in a stadium. How much fun would it be to watch the Super Bowl all alone in the stadium?"

"It'd be eerie." Travis raised his eyebrows.

"Being in a crowd gives us great joy. Also watching a good movie, enjoying the sunset on the beach, shopping, driving a fast car, good food —"

"Good sex," interrupted Travis with a mischievous look.

"That too," said Rishi, smiling. "And, many of us derive happiness from work."

"Sometimes," said Travis.

"Fine, not all of us. But many do, from scientists to artists, CEOs to doormen, people find great happiness in work. Then there are those who find happiness in service. You could gift them a Ferrari, but they'd find greater joy in serving others."

"Not me." Travis bobbed his head. "I'll take the Ferrari."

"I bet. We all find happiness in a different way and that's okay. Let's see… what am I missing… we find great happiness in our personal relationships, family, and friends. And, many of us find great happiness in faith."

Travis nodded.

"I might have missed some, but you get the sense of the different sources of happiness."

"Okay," said Travis, waiting for the punch line.

"But…."

"Yes." Travis motioned with his hand in anticipation.

"All these sources of happiness are also transient."

"You love that word, don't you?" Travis smiled.

"It's how life is," said Rishi, flipping his hand upwards. "These sources of happiness can stop giving us happiness at any time. For twenty years, I wanted to buy a Mercedes Benz S550. Suchi tells me I told her when I first met her."

"Did you?"

"Tell her?"

"No. Buy the car?" Travis widened his eyes.

"Yes, I did. Top of the line. Cost me over a hundred grand."

"Whoa!"

"I was in heaven the first time I drove it home." Rishi touched his chest. "Even if it was a horrible day at work, once I'd sit in the car, I'd forget everything. When we went on vacations, I couldn't wait to get home to drive it."

"How cool."

"Yeah, cool it was. Now, five years later, it's the same car, but the excitement has subsided."

"I don't buy that," said Travis.

"I'm telling you," said Rishi. "Now, I have a horrible day at work, I sit in the car, and the day's still horrible."

"Well...," said Travis.

"No matter the source of happiness...," Rishi paused to make sure Travis was completely attuned, "no matter the source of happiness, there's a possibility it could stop providing you happiness, or the level of happiness drops off."

Travis narrowed his eyes and followed closely.

"High-school sweethearts," said Rishi, "who have had a long happy marriage can still wake up one day and realize the love's gone. My neighbor's son wanted to be a doctor growing up. That's all he ever wanted. But once he got to college, he changed his mind overnight. People who've loved their line of work for years can still get tired of it even if they're making lots of money. People even lose their faith. It happens."

"True...," said Travis.

Rishi raised his index finger. "No matter the source of happiness," he paused for emphasis, "the receiver is always the mind — and the mind can change its preference without warning! That's a very important point to remember."

Travis narrowed his eyebrows. "What's the point again?"

"We could spend all our lives pursuing a source of happiness, and then all of a sudden it could stop satisfying our mind, leaving it disenchanted."

"True, but what's the point here... don't be happy?"

"No, no." Rishi waved his finger. "Enjoy the world and its pleasures, but don't ever make the mistake of assuming it's the real deal. If we want permanent happiness we need to look beyond the worldly sources, in fact...," Rishi slowed down, and in a hushed tone said, "we must look beyond our very mind!"

"Look beyond our mind." Travis shook his head. "Everything is beyond our mind. The soul is beyond our mind, and now our happiness is beyond our mind. Darn it!"

Rishi laughed. Travis did too.

"It is true, what can I say," said Rishi. "This is huuuuge!"

"Our poor mind. Fire the mind!" said Travis.

"The problem is people enjoying the material world don't appreciate the enormous, gigantic, tectonic importance of looking beyond their mind." Rishi raised his finger. "But the spiritual seekers know this is worth more than all the money in Las Vegas!"

"I was just teasing, I get it," said Travis. "The happiness our mind experiences is transient. We must go beyond the mind. That's why your muntruh emphasizes calming the mind."

Rishi smiled with great satisfaction. "Ah, very nice, thank you! Can you recite it?"

"Quiet your hungry mind, let your happy soul shine," said Travis.

Rishi repeated. "Quiet your hungry mind, let your happy soul shine." Rishi closed his eyes. "I wish this muntruh helps everyone." He opened his head and shook his head. "There's so much unnecessary pain and suffering in this world. Boy, I wish I could do something to help people."

"You are. You're talking to me."

Rishi smiled. "Maturing our perspectives reduces the material world's hold on us. It's like watching waves on an ocean. You see it as a play of nature. Similarly, once we mature, we see life itself as a play of the Universe. Then no matter what the circumstance we can remain stable and calmer."

"I guess it's easier said than done," said Travis, "it's difficult to snap your fingers and say, poof, I have a new perspective."

"True!" said Rishi. "Changing perspectives isn't easy. It's the same as making a lifestyle change. It takes a real commitment. The question to ask yourself, do I really want spiritual progress?"

Travis gave it a thought. "Everything you've said makes sense in theory. But, in practice, will we... become zombies?"

Rishi had a stern look. He did not like the word theory. "The spiritual method isn't an academic discussion. It's an absolutely practical way to live our lives in a much better way." Easing up Rishi said, "You won't be a zombie, au contraire, you'll be the life of the party, the go-to guy in the office."

Travis raised his eyebrows in skepticism.

"When your mind isn't perturbed by difficult circumstances, you're perpetually in a good mood," said Rishi. "Realistic in your assessment of situations because you're not overwhelmed by them, you'll be the best friend, non-judgmental, and always helping selflessly."

"Like you —"

"Kid, I have you fooled. If only you knew —"

"Knew what?"

"Never mind." Rishi waved his hand. "If you transform your thoughts and mature your perspectives, there won't be a gray day in your life. Actually, there will be gray days, but it won't affect your disposition. Your anxiety will go down."

Travis took it in silently. "My anxiety is sky high. I mean I can't even get my team to execute when I'm not there. "

Rishi looked caringly. "I know all about anxiety. If you quiet your mind, it'll help dissolve your anxiety. It'll help you manage better. Let's talk next how to quiet the mind."

"You better hurry before my mind explodes dealing with my team," said Travis.

Mature Your Perspectives

↑

There are no guarantees. Your life can change in a second.

Nothing in life is permanent. Everything you see will fade away.

Worldly happiness is temporary. Real, permanent happiness lies beyond your mind.

Developing a perspective of discernment and detachment is a powerful way to calm the mind.

Your problems may seem overwhelming now, but they will fade away with time. It is a law of life, all situations, good or bad, pass away.

Enjoy the world but do not make the mistake of assuming it is the real deal. If you want permanent happiness look beyond your own mind!

Chapter 15: Quiet Your Mind

Travis added, "My mind's working all the time. Huge quantity of thoughts. All the challenges, the stress."

"I'll share three exercises with you that I use to quiet my mind," said Rishi, "but before I do that, let's talk about the mind at a high level to set the context."

"Okay," said Travis.

Rishi extended his arm with curved fingers. "My brother-in-law once asked me, 'If you hold a glass of water for 10 minutes, what will happen.' I said, 'Nothing.' He said, 'What if you held it for a month?' He noted, 'Your arm will fall off.'"

"Got that right," said Travis. "Carrying even a small weight for a long time will kill us."

"Yet, we carry the heavy burden of stress for years," said Rishi.

"So, how do we put the glass of stress down?" asked Travis.

"Ever try to turn off your mind?" asked Rishi.

"Uh… didn't know I should, don't know how."

"Learning to do so can reduce stress and anxiety."

> *We all suffer from stress every day — for decades. That is catastrophic.*

"If I knew how, I'd turn it off for sure," said Travis.

"What happens when the day ends?" asked Rishi.

Nothing in this world is worth losing your internal peace.

"The Sun sets."

Rishi laughed. "No kidding. What's the end of your day?"

"I go to sleep."

"When you fall asleep this world simply dissolves." Rishi brought his hands together in slow motion.

"Uh… the world doesn't go anywhere," Travis shrugged, "just turning it off."

Rishi looked intently. "That's a profound statement!"

"What statement?" said Travis.

"Turning the world off, the world's your projection!"

"Whoa!" Travis leaned back with his palms raised. "My ego's not that big, I'm not the reason the world exists."

"Not a question of ego, without the perceiver the world cannot manifest itself."

"English please."

Rishi smiled. "A movie's running in the theater, but only when you go see it does it come alive for you. If there's no one to watch, it's as good as non-existent. No viewer, no world!"

"That'll take time to sink in," Travis's eyes wandered slowly, "…you're saying I turn on and off the world?"

"Every day, my friend… every day," said Rishi.

"If I turn it on, I should be able to disengage at will too."

"Now, you're talking, you're pretty smart," said Rishi clapping his hands. "You," he said emphasizing and pointing, "can walk out of the movie whenever you like."

"Sounds…," Travis wiggled his fingers, "…mysterious."

"I saw an IMAX movie once about high mountains and cliff drops over three thousand feet," said Rishi. "It was scary. I have fear of heights. As a prelude, they warned, this movie is very realistic, if you become afraid just close your eyes."

"So you'd close your eyes?" said Travis.

"Yes, and my fear would subside. You can close your eyes!"

Travis squinted. "Close my eyes?"

"Closing your eyes means giving your mind a break, disengaging it from the world. You engage with the world when you allow your mind to think about it. If you don't think about the world, you're disconnecting it."

"Intriguing…," said Travis.

"Imagine an investor decides not to invest in your company. Will you be upset?" asked Rishi.

"Better believe it," said Travis.

"But, if you don't think about it then it won't upset you."

Travis narrowed his eyes. "Nooo…."

"Yesss."

Travis thought about it. "…Okay, if I don't think about it then it won't bother me. But I'll keep thinking about it. And, not thinking about the problem won't make it go away."

"True, but you're limiting the impact of the problem. We reduce the amount of sunlight reaching our eyes by wearing shades. If we don't, sunlight will overwhelm us, and we won't see the landscape as well as we should. When we limit the thoughts, we can see the problem better and find solutions."

"Your points are sometimes hard to understand, but your analogies make it simple," said Travis. "Thank you."

"Sure. What do we do in a bad situation? We meet with friends, pray, or do some activity, allows us to take our mind away from what's bothering us. Gives us time to recharge."

"Stop one movie to play another," said Travis.

"That's an incredible capability we have and we use it instinctively," said Rishi. "You're in control of how much world you allow to come into your mind."

"That is… that's deep. You're in control of how much world you allow to come in," said Travis. "Boy, really need to appreciate this one. Wow!"

Rishi smiled in satisfaction. "People who are sucked into the world can't tell the difference between their mind and themselves," said Rishi.

Travis raised his eyebrows. "I can't tell the difference. Didn't know there was a difference."

"There is," said Rishi. "If you observe your thoughts, emotions, and habits, and put distance between you and your thoughts, you'll realize there's a big difference between you and your mind. Then you'll be able to turn off your mind at will."

Rishi pointed his finger at Travis. "You are not the mind." He looked intensely at Travis. "You — are not the mind!"

"Then who am I?"

With the flair of a wise master, Rishi said, "You are the owner of your mind! The boss of your mind."

Travis touched his forehead. "I like being the boss."

> *You are not the mind — you are the owner of the mind. Master your mind.*

"Our mind's like a big, unruly dog," said Rishi. "We have a leash, but we are unable to rein it in."

Travis listened with an amused look.

"Our job is to control this unruly dog, train it, make it do our bidding, and become its master. Right now we're the slave."

"It'll be great to pull the leash on the mind," said Travis.

Rishi was relishing the discussion. "You must have an out-of-mind experience, observe how your mind thinks. You'll be surprised how your mind sometimes reacts in ways that are completely opposite to what you believe, and who you are."

"Oh, many times, I can't believe how I act," said Travis.

"We must learn the ability to live outside the mind and watch it. Become mind-aware," said Rishi.

"Wow, quite a concept! I haven't heard the term mind-aware before, but I see the value, it's like mindfulness."

Rishi wrinkled his nose. "Actually, I want to head towards — mindlessness."

Travis took a moment. "Of course. That's a good one."

"Most of the time, when thoughts arise, we're fully engaged with those thoughts. But as you become mind-aware you'll be able to choose whether you want to engage or let it dissolve."

"Interesting," said Travis amused.

"Yes, I do it all the time, well... not all the time, but often."

"What do you do?" asked Travis.

"I, at least when I'm in a calmer state, observe as thoughts arise in my mind and then check myself and not let the thought grow. Soon enough the thought disappears."

"And then?" asked Travis.

"I experience a bit of silence, before the next one surfaces."

"As if they're waves on the ocean," said Travis.

"Great analogy, thoughts constantly rise and dissolve."

"You do this while you sit for meditation?" asked Travis.

"Certainly when I sit for meditation, but even when I'm going about my daily life," said Rishi. "I'll get a thought about someone or something, I'll recognize it's not pleasing, and I tell myself to not feed it, just let it go away. And it does!"

"That's really cool," said Travis.

"Well, it'd be cool if I was able to do it all the time. There are times when I can get stressed and caught up in the thought-storm, but sometimes I'm able to walk back and protect myself from being sucked into the whirlwind."

"I'd like to be able to do that," said Travis.

"You will. The first thing you must do is recognize engaging a thought is a choice you have. You can say no thank you to a thought. Say to yourself, I'm not going to do that."

"Not do what?" said Travis.

"Not give fuel to that thought."

"Can I stop the thought from arising?" asked Travis.

"Well, sort of. In the beginning, you consciously chose if you encourage a thought or not. Over time, the thoughts that you starve will show up less often. They'll stop arising."

"We did talk about that, thoughts feed on themselves."

"Right," said Rishi, "so if you cut off the supply, that chain of thoughts will shrink. It works. One of my bosses had taken advantage of me. I was hurt deeply. I spend months hating him until I realized nothing was happening to him, I was the one suffering. I needed to stop that chain of thoughts. I decided, whenever I think about him, I'll cut it off. It took discipline and time, but I broke free and the matter had a lesser hold on me."

"It's as if you forgave him," said Travis.

"Forgiving is powerful, but in this case, I don't think I forgave him, even though I should have. I just stopped thinking about it. The scar is there, but the wound has healed."

"Can we do this with all thoughts?" asked Travis.

"Yes. Scuttle all bad thoughts… even good thoughts."

Travis tapped his thumb. "Why would I do that?"

"Say, you have a thought about an investor who's likely to fund your business. It's a good thought and you keep playing it in your mind. It makes you happy."

Travis smiled.

"See, you're smiling."

Travis grinned even further.

"Even such thoughts can cause a problem. It's setting up expectations and anticipation deep inside you."

"I could be setting myself up for disappointment?"

Rishi nodded.

"But isn't it silly not to enjoy good thoughts?"

"Ah, there's the rub," said Rishi. "The enjoyment of thoughts or the enjoyment that comes from thoughts is always fleeting because situations change and thoughts change. The real, true, everlasting enjoyment is in the absence of thoughts!"

"Have to get used to that one," said Travis.

"I know it's radical. Our modern day life is frenzied and overworked. We're on the go all the time, constantly busy —"

"Never-ending," said Travis.

"We're bombarded by TVs, computers, phones. The mind is overstimulated. Being on constantly robs our peace."

Travis nodded.

"If you slow down thoughts, your quality of life will improve. You'll enjoy your blessings — your family, friends, food, movies, everything will be richer."

"Umm...," muttered Travis.

"Right now as you frenziedly go through your days, every life experience is a big blur. You'll wake up one day and wonder where the years went. When did I become old? When did my charming and beautiful wife stop being charming and what did I do to cause that? When did I stop enjoying the simpler things in life, when did I become shallow and superficial? When did I stop being a friend? When did I stop loving myself?"

"You're scaring me," said Travis.

"Sorry, don't mean to. Slow down the constant tsunami of thoughts, then life will shine, you'll get a glimpse of heaven. Real heaven is not out there in cosmic space, it's right here — in you!"

> *The real heaven is not out there in cosmic space, it is in — You!*

"Life is going by... I'm in a funk," said Travis.

"I know, that's why we must transform our lives," said Rishi. "Quieting our minds is the best way to do it. Can you recite the muntruh for me please?"

"Quiet my mind, let my soul shine."

"Good job. To quiet the mind we must learn to manage it, not fight it or punish it, but intelligently manage it."

"How?" asked Travis.

"May I share a story?"

"Please." Travis smiled.

"A king had a very difficult horse. His best trainers failed to tame it. They'd try to mount the horse but get thrown off."

"Okay," said Travis. "I like your stories."

Rishi smiled. "Ultimately, the king announced a reward. But, no one came forward. No one wanted their bones broken." Travis chuckled.

"The king gave up. Then a young boy came forward and said he'll train the horse. His only condition, he needed a lot of time. People laughed at the boy."

'Then?"

"Having no other option, the king decided to take a chance. Months went by, the king didn't hear back. He wondered if the horse had died and the lad had run away. Then one day the boy arrived in court and requested the king to come out."

"Where was the horse?" asked Travis.

"Outside. As the king and his courtiers went out, the boy effortlessly mounted the horse and gracefully paraded the horse around the palace grounds. Everyone was stunned."

"How did he do it?"

"Exactly what the king asked. The boy replied, 'Your majesty, your people made the mistake of forcing the horse. I let it be itself at my ranch. I let it run, and I'd run along when it ran. I let it eat all it wanted and I'd eat at the same time. I let it sleep all it wanted and I'd sleep at the same time. Soon the horse believed I was its friend and allowed me to train it.'"

"Wow," said Travis.

"Our mind is like the horse, we can't win if we force it. The more we force the more it rebels. Therefore, I'm not a fan of religious doctrines that advocate strict penance and austerity."

"Treat it gently," said Travis.

"Yes. Then it'll drop its resistance. It'll take time but it'll happen."

"Lot of time?" asked Travis.

"Yes," said Rishi, "we live in times of instant gratification, people go to one retreat and want immediate nirvana. Sit for meditation once and want the mind to calm down instantly. We have millions of impressions from previous thoughts, feelings, actions, and habits, they must be neutralized."

"Talking about habits, have you conquered temptations?"

Rishi laughed. "First, I don't call them temptations or vices. I don't like to judge. But, I do indulge in pleasures."

"Like?"

"Man, you're pushy."

Travis pulled back.

"It's all right," said Rishi, "I'll answer. I enjoy drinking, I like sex, I love to make money and succeed, I'm highly competitive, what else... I love to eat, I like to have a good time. And, I have serious anger issues."

Travis waited.

"That's all." Rishi threw hands up. "Sorry, for my indiscretions... I'm human."

"Nothing wrong with what you've shared," said Travis.

"Well... that's all I'm disclosing," said Rishi with a grin.

"I know you, you're a good man." Travis gave a firm nod.

Rishi laughed. "You say that even after my confession."

"Yup," said Travis. "Your temptations... do you have to become purer... to make progress in finding happiness?"

"I've wondered myself, but, if you remember spirituality doesn't discriminate," said Rishi.

"Yup, we did talk about that," said Travis.

"My hope is spirituality won't deny me in spite of my habits," said Rishi. "Sometimes, religions advise become a monk, practice celibacy, live minimally, spend your time in devotional activities. They're right to a certain extent. These things will help quiet your mind," Rishi tapped the sofa, "but they aren't always sufficient."

"Because your mind can still wonder?" said Travis.

"Yes, if you can train your mind to become quieter, you can live in this world, enjoy all its joys and pleasures and still achieve spirituality. That's my thesis… and my life's journey depends on it." Rishi touched his heart.

"Don't worry." Travis did a thumbs up. "It'll work."

"I sure hope so. Religion asks people to give up everything. That's not practical. It works for a subset of the population who can become a priest or a monk. But doesn't work for the majority. I'm looking for something that works for everyone."

"I like that," said Travis.

"If we transform our thoughts, mature our perspectives, and quiet our minds, spirituality will automatically manifest. I believe that, and I experience that."

Travis smiled. "Okay, how do we quiet the mind?"

"Quieting the mind has two phases. In the first phase, you need to slow the mind. In the second phase, you meditate deeply, where the thoughts stop."

"Wow," said Travis.

"Yeah, good stuff. Let's talk about slowing the mind. "If you don't slow the mind, you'll find meditation is frustrating."

"Okay," said Travis.

"I try to do two exercises every day. And, I engage in a third exercise on weekends. These disengage my mind from the world, and reduce my state of frenzy."

"I'd like to learn them," said Travis.

"Sure, they're simple but highly effective. You just have to remember to do them consistently. That's the only catch."

"Which is the first exercise?" asked Travis.

"Mind purge," said Rishi, "also called the recliner exercise."

Travis smiled.

Rishi smiled too. "I sit in my recliner and turn off all the distractions. Then I let my mind think through whatever it wants to. When a thought comes up, I don't engage it, I let it play out. If I remember I have a meeting the next day, I don't start thinking about preparing for the meeting."

"You sit there and let things go through your mind."

"Yeah. I just let it flow through," said Rishi. "It allows my mind to process everything it's consumed during the day."

"Okay, then what happens?" said Travis.

"After about 15 to 20 minutes, my mind has regurgitated all its thoughts and emotions and runs out of things to think about. Of course, I'm describing a routine day, if something catastrophic happened the mind would just go on and on."

"Understand that. On a routine day —"

"My mind is done and I feel really relaxed. Just like our body processes all the food we eat, our mind also needs to process the day's happenings. I find the mind purge is very useful. I sleep better on the days I go through this exercise."

"I can't imagine my mind will quiet down even in an hour," said Travis, "it'll go on and on."

"Yes, that's possible the first time you do it, and maybe for the first month. But eventually, you'll get to the point where 15 to 20 minutes might be sufficient to purge the mind."

"When do you do it?" asked Travis.

"Sometimes before I leave office, or I'll do it as soon as I get home. When I do it, I find I'm more engaged with my family, I'm calmer, and enjoy the evening fully."

"Can I do it before I go to bed?" asked Travis.

"You can but it can backfire," said Rishi.

"Why?" asked Travis.

"Somedays, your mind is able to exhaust its thoughts and you'll feel sleepy," said Rishi. "Occasionally, the thoughts are so virulent, they agitate you more and spoil your sleep. So I like to purge my mind at least a couple of hours before I sleep."

"I'll keep that in mind," said Travis.

"Let me share an exercise that helps me sleep soundly."

"Oh, good." Travis leaned forward.

"I call it the thought-massage," said Rishi.

"The what?"

"Massaging your body with thought," said Rishi.

"How quaint," said Travis.

Rishi smiled. "This really works when I've done the mind purge previously. I lie down on my back and stretch my hands out slightly with my palms facing upward. I close my eyes and slowly focus on every part of my body, starting from my head to my feet. I pay attention for a few seconds to all parts, including my eyes, ears, throat, chest, stomach, arms, fingers, palms, basically every inch of my body."

"Okay, then?"

"As I do this, in a few minutes I feel my entire body relax, feel my nerves and muscles relax. Then before I even know it, I've fallen asleep. It works wonderfully for me. Try it."

"I will," said Travis.

"The simple combination of a mind purge and a thought massage daily is a wonderful antidote for me. Then on the weekends, I engage in some nothing-time," said Rishi.

Travis smiled. "That's interesting. What's nothing-time?"

"I spend time doing nothing! I just sit for an hour in my backyard, casually observing the birds and the clouds, the small waves in the lake. I always come away refreshed."

"I'm a doer. I have to be doing something," said Travis. "I just can't sit down doing nothing."

"Try it! The ability do nothing is an incredible gift. Our minds want constant stimulation, being able to take it down a notch and let it drift is amazing. Of course, you can do it in a park, on the beach, at home, wherever you feel peaceful."

"What about exercising? Calms me down," said Travis.

"Exercising still involves interaction with machines or your own thoughts about how the exercise session is progressing," said Rishi. "I like to go for walks. Walking is calming, but I still find my mind's racing as I walk. Being stationary works best for me. Exercising, sports, help, but I find I need a stronger and deeper dose of disengagement."

> *Do you know who is your best friend? It is your own self! Spend time with your own self daily. It will never leave your side.*

"I guess reading a book is not nothing-time," said Travis.

"Not really. Reading engages you in a different direction," said Rishi. "Be in nature by yourself without distractions. Be in a place of worship with no distractions. For many people, faith and devotion can be very powerful in calming their mind. People feel closer to God in a place of worship because their minds calm down and they experience a glimmer of their soul," said Rishi. "In Sanskrit, a temple is called mundir. It means where the mind is still. Other ways to calm down, take a bath in a hot tub, or water plants with a hose."

"That can get really boring," said Travis.

"Sure," said Rishi, "sitting still can be boring if you have an overactive mind. But, you'll come to enjoy it with time. Persist and you'll relish it. Whenever I do the mind purge, the thought massage, and the nothing-time activities regularly, it puts me in a peaceful mood, making it ripe for my meditation session."

"All right," said Travis. "When do you do meditation?"

"In the mornings. On the weekends, I'll do it a second time during the afternoon or evening."

"So how do you do meditation?" asked Travis.

"Let's discuss meditation in a few minutes. I want to share more aspects about quieting the mind."

"Sure," said Travis.

"Quieting the mind's not a one day project. Do it every day. Then you'll become peaceful, and you will notice anxiety will slowly but surely dissolve."

"What if you try for years and still don't become peaceful?"

"It's possible you're so deeply consumed with the world, any progress seems minimal," said Rishi. "It can be discouraging, but remember, don't keep expectations. Do it because it's the main purpose of your life, not because you can't wait to see the results."

Travis listened.

Rishi pressed on, "As you do more spiritual practice, it'll push back the other distractions of life."

"It'll make room for itself?" said Travis as he smiled.

"Yes, indeed. The other aspects of life, fame, fortune, relationships, may still matter, but with lesser and lesser intensity. In fact, you'll be able to develop a discerning capability. You'll engage with them but they won't have a strong hold on you."

"Spirituality will fill my life, diminishing the other aspects?" asked Travis.

"Yes, you have it," said Rishi.

"I'll try the exercises," said Travis, "but often I don't make it home till late. I don't think I have the time to do all of that."

Rishi bristled. "Ah… we take the time to go to the gym because we understand the value of strengthening our body, but we don't give our mind the same level of importance. Strengthening the mind may be a million times more important than physical health. People say health is wealth. That's true, but internal peace is the most precious wealth."

"Fine, I'll make time, interrupt work in the evenings —"

> *Internal peace is the most precious wealth.*

"You got this wrong," said Rishi.

"What do you mean?"

"Flip your perspective," said Rishi. "The mind purge is not the interruption, your work is the interruption in your spiritual quest. Spirituality should be your highest priority, otherwise achieving peace will only be a distant goal."

Travis shook his head. "I have deadlines… meetings."

"Yup, I know," said Rishi curling his lips. "I've been there, I've given the world higher priority and all it did was take my life to the edge of crisis. Only when I started quieting my mind was I able to walk back from the cliff."

Travis struggled.

"Listen, I've shared with you the most profound spiritual knowledge, but that knowledge is utterly useless, a complete waste if you won't make the effort," said Rishi in a stern, resigned tone. "Try to do the mind purge consistently, it'll make you far more productive at work. The improvement in your productivity and decision making," Rishi snapped his fingers, "will outstrip the little time you put into these exercises."

"I believe that," said Travis in an appreciative tone. "I don't question it. I struggle if I'll stick to it."

"Can't help you there, I've had problems myself." Rishi snapped his fingers. "Maybe that's the saving grace. I haven't been consistent but still, the benefits are there. Whenever I get back into the routine, I feel calmer."

Travis listened.

Rishi said, "You may feel calmer in two days, or two hundred days, I don't know, the point is whenever you do it, it'll produce results."

"Okay," said Travis half-heartedly.

Rishi did his best to sell. "And, if like me, you drop off, then sooner or later you'll get frustrated with the world and it'll be your cue to start calming your mind. Even if you have to take steps back, you'll be much better off having pushed forward."

Travis was noncommittal. It bothered Rishi.

We are not the mind!
Withdraw from the mind
to discover the Heaven within You!

**Quiet
Your Mind**

Control "how much
world" you allow into
your mind. Learn to turn
off the world.

Purge the mind daily.
This will allow your mind
to breathe and it will
improve your mood.

Engage in "Nothing-
Time" activities on
weekends. Over time a
sense of wellbeing will
embrace you.

Faith and devotion are
powerful in their ability
to calm the mind.

Meditate daily. There is
nothing more important!
If you don't have time,
at least close your eyes
and be calm while
traveling, or between
tasks during the day.

Chapter 16: Workplace

Rishi decided to delve further into Travis's mind. Gesturing in a circular fashion, Rishi asked, "Do you feel like a hamster in the rotating wheel at work? Working all the time, non-stop."

"It's a startup." Travis nudged his head. "If I don't put in the time, it'll never take off."

"You think about the company all the time?"

"24/7!"

"Even when you're with Cindi?"

"She understands. Sacrifices, man!"

Rishi looked down.

Travis narrowed his shoulders. "Listen, I get it, my mind's consumed with Travisto. But it takes that, it needs that."

Rishi felt disappointed with Travis's cursory dismissal. He wondered if Travis had gone along with the whole discussion at a superficial level and was not going to make a concerted effort to change his thinking. Rishi asked, "Do you enjoy your work?"

"I... well, sometimes."

Rishi asked, "Why sometimes?"

"Sometimes it's just frustrating."

"When your software programmers put bugs in the code?"

Travis squirmed.

Rishi pushed Travis's buttons. "When investors don't invest?"

Travis looked away.

Rishi looked intently. "When customers refuse to see the value proposition?"

"Going to roast me on the coals next?" said Travis as he twisted his arm back and forth.

Rishi laughed. "No. Imagine Michelangelo or Einstein working, and you working. What's the difference?"

"…They didn't have to worry about raising money."

"And…," said Rishi.

"Not worry about customers… I don't know," said Travis.

Rishi said, "I've a feeling they did their work without expectations of success or failure, remember we talked about that?"

"Yup."

Rishi said, "Because they did their work with a calm mind, they were always in their zone. When we're frustrated and anxious —"

"I know that! How do I fix it?" said Travis.

"By removing fear. When you're afraid of the outcome… do you remember the point about not focusing on outcomes?"

"Yeah, love the effort, not the outcome," said Travis. "But now I'm in the real world, if the investors don't invest next week, we could go belly up… maybe not quite. We're in a tough spot… our last round of funding was three long years ago. We're running low on funds." Travis clamped his fist. "It's so frustrating."

"Your mind's fearful, it's consumed with finding a break."

"I can't give up on my dreams… my team's counting on me." Travis shook his head. "I keep letting them down."

Rishi took a deep breath. He looked down at the carpet and moved his fingers along the edge of the sofa. "This may sound Latin to you, but you could be your own biggest enemy."

Travis grimaced.

"Our mind can be our best friend or our worst enemy," said Rishi. "With a stable mind, we can accomplish what we desire. Your fear and self-pressure is your greatest enemy."

Travis dug his thumbnail into his arm.

"You have so much pressure," said Rishi, "I bet you go to meetings so obsessed with your need for funding you're not listening well to the investors. In your preoccupations, you're truly not understanding what they're asking, not recognizing what they're seeking."

Our mind can be our
best friend,
or our worst enemy.

Travis's face turned pale.

"Is it?" probed Rishi, turning business coach.

Travis squirmed. "I'm listening to them."

"As well as you could? The first rule of sales is to listen and focus on the prospect and not be preoccupied with what you want."

Travis did not answer.

"Why aren't investors biting?" probed Rishi. "How many presentations have you made?"

"At least 20."

"Why aren't they biting?"

"Wish I knew." Travis exhaled.

"You know it," said Rishi pointing in Travis's direction. "Calm down and search your mind. You've heard the objections, the pushbacks, you've seen their body language change as you've answered questions. Search. The answer is in you. How's the presentation next week going to be different?" said Rishi.

Travis struggled. "More —"

"More features and functionality in your apps?" said Rishi.

"Well...." Travis scanned the floor.

"You know that's not the answer," said Rishi.

Travis squeezed his hand. "I... well... sorta...."

Rishi leaned forward. "Then, why focus on adding more features?"

"How do you know, Rishi?" Travis looked surprised.

"It's a hunch, Travis. I know you. I remember the trouble you were having before I had you join my team at Ixsor."

Travis felt his energy drain.

"Travis, you've never understood yourself. You're the consummate engineer, a perfectionist in love with your creations. You don't want to sell. You believe investors should see value in Travisto because your apps are so perfect. But no investor cares about the apps as much as you do. They want to know how the business will accelerate. They want to find out if you're a businessman or a technologist. Am I wrong?"

"No." Travis lowered his eyes.

"Is that what's happening with Travisto? I used to give you candid feedback, is that the reason you didn't stay in touch?"

"Nooo." Travis looked away as if Rishi had caught his secret. Travis ran his hands through his thick hair. "I don't know Rishi, I don't know. I'm trying so hard."

Rishi said in a reassuring tone, "Remember, we talked about becoming mind-aware. Understand how your mind works, and then you'll see how you might be your biggest obstacle."

"How...." Travis's breathing became heavy. "How do I?"

"First, accept you're a perfectionist who likes to tinker with things," said Rishi. "But that's not what's required from a CEO. Either hire a CEO or channel yourself by working on the product only 20% of the time and 80% on managing the company."

"But working on the product gives me peace and joy. It's my escape… my oasis."

"Your true oasis is a peaceful mind," said Rishi. "Product development gives you relief, but it's temporary, as soon as you're called to do other things, you despise it and it makes life hell for you."

Rishi was reading Travis like a book. On the verge of breaking down, Travis quivered. "I hate all this other stuff I've to do as CEO, drives me nuts and sucks the very life and energy out of me. I hate selling."

"Then why do it?"

"Because I have to, there's no one else, I'm a small company," said Travis in a derisive tone.

"Stop torturing yourself," said Rishi, as if he was holding Travis by his shoulders. "Understand your strengths and focus on them. Don't fight yourself." Rishi paused. "Do you have a salesperson on the team?"

"No."

"Hire one."

"Can't afford one," promptly came Travis's reply.

"Then partner with one or hire one on a commission or equity basis. Let them do the selling to investors and customers," advised Rishi.

"But they won't have the conviction," said Travis. "You know this, founders are the best salespeople."

In his mentoring tone, Rishi said, "Don't get caught up in everything you've heard. It's true, many founders are great at selling, but don't hold yourself to others' standards." Rishi leaned forward. "I'll say again, understand your strengths and weaknesses."

"Okay," said Travis listening as if his life depended on it.

"I'm not saying don't go to a sales call. Go, but let someone else do the grunt work. In the sales meetings, let your salesperson make the presentation. Then, when clients turn to you, whatever you say as the founder will be authoritative. You might enjoy that."

"I really like that," said Travis, his energy spiking.

"Why?" asked Rishi.

"I'm a straight-shooter, I can't answer diplomatically, my abruptness is a turn-off. I see eyes roll when I get too technical. A salesperson could do the schmoozing. It could be a win-win."

Rishi smiled.

Travis spent a few minutes thinking. He stood up and extended his hand. "Thank you!" Rishi shook hands while continuing to sit. Travis sat down and finished off his water.

"Some more?" asked Rishi.

"No thanks."

"I bet your team's stressed too," said Rishi. "You need to work on your stress and theirs too. Happy and stress-free workers are far more productive than stressed workers."

"Stress elevates focus," said Travis.

"In the short term, yes, but in the long term, a happy team will beat the pants off a perennially stressed team."

Travis tapped his thumb. "Some amount of stress is necessary."

"No, it's not. You've got to change your corporate culture."

"We'll worry about the culture once we get funding." Travis flipped his hand dismissively.

Rishi did not like the answer and the gesture. He stood up to stretch his legs. He walked over to the windows, and slowly paced along the windows looking out.

Travis stole a glance at his emails. He gritted his teeth in frustration and was about to reply when Rishi said, "One of my challenges is to transform my company."

Travis put the phone down. "In what way?"

Rishi replied, "The corporate culture at Hinteq —"

"Sucks?" said Travis.

Rishi grimaced. "Yes, it does, and that bothers me. Workplaces have such an uninviting, watch-your-back culture. In all my years in the corporate world, one thing that's struck me is how internal politics plague the workplace."

"Hated it! That's why I prefer a small firm," said Travis.

"Sure, but as Travisto grows you'll have your share of it."

"We'll fight it." Travis closed his fist.

"It's a tough fight. I have over two thousand consultants in my delivery team. So it's a bit of a challenge for me," said Rishi.

"Whoa, didn't realize that many people report to you! How are you going to change them? You were very good at Ixsor, you cut the crap, saved my butt from being thrown out."

"Wish I could've done more," said Rishi. "Scott loved creating internal tension between teams. He felt it brought out the edge in people. I expected a lot more from him as a CEO."

"He was a jerk," said Travis with a dirty scorn.

"Now, now." Rishi took his seat.

"He was," said Travis in a determined tone.

"Well," said Rishi, "he was super competitive and wanted everyone else to be the same. Scott's problem was he lacked empathy. He wanted growth and didn't care if people burnt-out. That troubled me." Rishi shook his head. "I tried to convince him otherwise, but I failed."

"So what're you telling your troops?" asked Travis.

"We're in a competitive market," said Rishi. "Clients treat our services as commodities."

"Doesn't sound like fun," said Travis.

"It isn't." Rishi sighed. "Hinteq acts like a body shop, and then my peers wonder why our people have no loyalty. If the economy softens, we're happy to let them go at the drop of a hat. We have become so transactional in our thinking."

"It's capitalism, man."

"It's ineffective capitalism," said Rishi. "We spend so much of our lives at work, and yet we've stripped away human values. I'm trying to get management to start caring. Care about our people, they're not numbers on a spreadsheet, they're souls."

Rishi slowed. "I told them, we the management team are creating a shallow, superficial organization, and we're becoming shallow and superficial ourselves."

"What did they say?"

"My boss Vera, the CEO, is a very nice woman, she's responding. The rest of the team is super cautious because they fear it'll hurt the business."

"Won't it hurt the business?" asked Travis.

"Not if I can help it," said Rishi. "If the management team genuinely cares, our team members will recognize that. Then, we can ask them to care —"

"For themselves?" said Travis.

"Care for the customers. Because we're in this cutthroat business, we don't care for our clients, and because our clients see us a necessary evil, they don't care for us. It's a mechanical, transactional relationship."

Travis moved his hand through his hair. "Will caring make more money?"

"No. Clients won't pay us more or negotiate less because we care," said Rishi.

"Then it's a waste of time," said Travis wearing his CEO hat.

"If we care, it'll reduce stress and anxiety in Hinteq. Slowly it'll lead to stronger relationships. My message to clients at the conference was, we'll genuinely care for you, and you must care for us. Let's get past transactional relationships, let's form a partnership."

"And the response?" asked Travis.

"They liked it," said Rishi.

"Seriously? The touchy-feely stuff?"

"Yes. What's awesome is so many of them said until now no executive from Hinteq had been so open about the issues and acknowledged what was missing from the relationship."

"You sure, they weren't just being polite?" said Travis.

Rishi narrowed his brow. "I hope not." He touched his chest. "We're spiritual beings, and we spend so much of our lives at work, we must treat each other right."

"Is that utopian?" said Travis. "Accountability and profits are important." Travis's phone vibrated, but he ignored it.

"Of course they are, but so is the culture. We must change our workplace culture," said Rishi. "I need to do it in my company, you need to do it in Travisto."

Travis stood up abruptly and walked to the windows. Rishi felt something was amiss. Travis held the sheer curtains between his fingers, moving his fingers back and forth rapidly, as he continued looking out.

Then Travis turned to look at Rishi, his face red. Rishi asked, "Everything okay?"

Travis took a moment to answer. In a heavy tone, he said, "Rishi, I appreciate all this talk about corporate culture and all the discussion about spirituality, but…."

Rishi went, oh, no, in his mind. "But, what…," said Rishi, as calmly as he could, disguising his apprehension.

Travis shook his head. "I can't do this."

"What do you mean? Do what?" said Rishi.

"All this caring in the workplace, too touchy-feely for me." Travis's voice and conviction picked up. "I don't have the time to do all of this. I can't… I really can't… turn away from my company… I appreciate the feedback on hiring a salesperson and the other stuff, I like the ideas, I'll implement them… but I'm realizing… I'm not ready for spirituality." He shook his head. "This isn't the right time. Travisto needs me. Maybe later."

Rishi was stunned.

Travis walked back and sat on the sofa. He felt relieved as if he had lifted a weight off his shoulders. Rishi, on the other hand, felt Travis had dropped a bomb.

We spend so much of our life at work, try your best to create a happy environment for you and your co-workers.

Chapter 17: Confession

Rishi sat frozen. Breathing heavily, Travis scanned the rug. It was a stalemate. Travis looked up. "I'm sorry, buddy."

Rishi didn't respond, his face shell-shocked. Then he closed his eyes and calmed himself. He took several deep breaths. A faint smile broke out and his face relaxed.

Rishi opened his eyes and surveyed Travis, who was in visible discomfort. In a soothing voice, Rishi said, "You wanted to learn about spirituality."

Travis looked up with guilt on his face. "Yes, I wanted spirituality, I want spirituality... but timing isn't right. I must focus on Travisto. That's foremost. I must get my team to deliver. They're not getting it." Travis shook his head.

Rishi closed his eyes briefly. Then he said, "Travis, I've dabbled with spirituality all my life, but never pursued it seriously until the last year and a half." He looked intensely. "I used to think like you, I don't have the time, other things are more important. I had all the spiritual knowledge but I was putting in very little time practicing spirituality. Acquiring wisdom and knowledge without acting on it is a waste of time."

Travis listened, not sure he wanted to hear all of that. He seemed to have made his mind up. Rishi watched Travis pull his body up, a sign he was ready to leave. Rishi lifted his palms to stall him. Rishi said, "You've got to learn from my terrible mistakes. I'm such a miserable person and if it wasn't for —"

"Why, Rishi? Why? Why do you put yourself down? What is it? What could you've done to have such a low opinion of yourself? I don't want spirituality now, big deal. Why do you have to put yourself down?"

Rishi folded his arms across his chest and looked down, his eyes moving rapidly. He looked disturbed.

Travis was not sure what was going on. "Rishi —"

"I need to…," said Rishi in a defeated tone, "share my story so you can understand how our minds can ruin our lives. If I hadn't turned to spirituality, I wouldn't have been around…."

"What do you mean?"

"…Two years ago I lost my job. We had scheduled Priya's wedding in nine months. We consider it a sacred duty to give your daughter in wedding. Plus, she was getting married in India, which made it complex."

Travis did not want to hear the story, but out of respect for Rishi, he engaged. "Why India?"

"I wanted her to marry someone from Houston, but life had its own plans. She was visiting India with Suchi for a cousin's wedding. She met a boy who's the son of Suchi's friend from high school. They liked each other. We were happy, we know the family well, and it all fell into place."

"Sounds great," said Travis.

"Well… we had saved money for Priya's wedding, but now we needed a lot more. In India, often, the entire wedding costs are borne by the bride's family. Plus, the boy's family is super rich, and so Suchi and I wanted to throw a grand wedding for our only daughter."

"Sure."

"The costs are incredible," said Rishi, "a five-day event with multiple functions and parties, trousseau for Priya with dresses, purses, shoes, and sets of jewelry. The gifts for the in-laws and their extended family. We bought our son-in-law a BMW."

"I should've married an Indian girl." Travis smiled.

"You should've. Weddings in Mumbai are so over-the-top, so much excess. Plus the number of extended family and relatives, and friends. We had five hundred people from the groom's side and three hundred from our side."

Travis raised his eyebrows. "You serious?"

"Oh, yes. Our budget was seriously out of control. And, of course, I had a little problem, no job. I knew only one place where I could make some money fast."

Travis shook his head. "Oh, no."

"I borrowed on margin to add funds to my stock investments."

"Then?" asked Travis.

"For two months things were great, I was trading daily, I had the time as I was out of work. I felt the job loss was a blessing. I figured I'd make much more managing my money than working somewhere. I was hoping to double the money."

"Did it crash?"

Rishi rolled his eyes. "Bigtime. There was bad news from China about its economy, the market crashed overnight. I had bought options. In options trading, if you're making money, you can make a lot, but if you lose, you lose big. I got killed."

"Oh, my!"

Rishi squeezed the pillow hard. "I panicked big." He grimaced. "Couldn't think straight, sold the positions for sixty percent loss, fearing the crash was going to get worse. The talking heads on TV made it sound as if the world was ending."

Rishi looked up at the ceiling, reliving every moment of it. "How much did you lose?" asked Travis.

"Twenty years of savings wiped out," his eyes moved side to side, "over… nine hundred thousand dollars!"

"Oh, my God!" said Travis as he jerked up. "That's a chunk. That's a lot of money," he said widening his eyes.

Rishi's face contorted, he grabbed the pillow, put it on his lap, and wrapped his hands around it. He never discussed how much money he had with anyone. He had violated his rule. He froze like a rabbit in the garden caught eating.

"That's a lot of money. You wanted more? Double it?"

Rishi turned red, not liking the inquisition.

"If you had that much," Travis quickly did the math, "it must've been around one and a half million. Why feel inadequate? Wasn't that enough?"

Rishi pushed back firmly. "What are you hoping to earn?"

"Don't know."

"Hundred million? More?" said Rishi.

Travis bobbed his head. "But…."

"But, what?"

"That's far-fetched," said Travis. "Five years in the startup and still I draw no salary. California is expensive. Living in an apartment on Cindi's salary. We have barely fifteen thousand in the bank," said Travis sharing without hesitation. "You had thousand times what we have, wait… a hundred times."

Rishi felt bad, having no inkling of how much money Travis had. "Sorry, I shouldn't have brought up money."

"I don't mind discussing it, as you say, it is what it is," said Travis. "You had talked about an investor who lost $13 million. That wasn't a hypothetical story, that is you, isn't it?"

Rishi's face turned pale. His lips quivering, he said, "I can't describe the devastation I felt." His voice trailed off. "That knot in the stomach, that abject and absolute helplessness. I'd be in the house and feel trapped as if the walls were caving on me."

"I felt that with Nathan," said Travis, his face contorted. It made him realize pain can come in different forms. "Sorry for your loss, I'm glad it was just money."

"That wasn't the worst of it," said Rishi.

"What could be worse?"

"Now, there was no money to throw the grand wedding."

"Did you spend your daughter's wedding funds too?"

"No, never. Would've surely killed myself if I'd done that."

"That's a relief," said Travis.

"Well...."

"Well, what?"

"Suchi still wanted to have a grand wedding for Priya. All her family was going to be there, her old friends. She didn't want Priya's wedding to be any less because of my screw up."

"But where's the money?" asked Travis.

"She had a solution," replied Rishi. "She asked her rich brothers who were more than happy to help. In India, brothers will happily step in, especially if it's a daughter's wedding. It's considered a noble deed. Not to mention they're so wealthy this was pocket change."

"Good."

Rishi grimaced. "Nope, not good."

"Why?"

"This was my daughter's wedding, and I couldn't imagine taking a cent from her brothers. That'd hurt my self-esteem."

"Your ego, it would hurt your ego."

"It's not about ego, it's...." Rishi looked away.

Travis didn't say anything, just shook his head a little.

"As a father, it's my responsibility…," said Rishi, his eyes moistening up, "what kind of a father I am if I can't give my daughter a nice wedding, my only daughter."

"But you had the money you saved for the wedding."

"That's what I told my wife, we'll do a good wedding, it won't be grand, and we can scale back on the invitees. But she wouldn't have it. She said in India it's very difficult not to invite people. It's a close-knit society, everyone knows everyone, and everyone knows everything. Not inviting people, she argued, would be highly disrespectful and insulting. She saw no problem in taking help from her brothers and said no one had to know. The problem I told her was that I'd know. It would rob me of my joy, rob me of my pride."

"She agreed?"

"No. She said the wedding was not about me, it was about our daughter and that should be the only focus. I was mad, upset at her, but excruciatingly upset with myself. I hated myself. Didn't know if I should bang my head on the walls."

Travis wrinkled his face. "Weren't you overreacting a bit?"

Rishi closed his eyes. "…Watching the wedding preparations became a slow and terrible torture. The joy of my daughter's wedding turned into such a horrible pain. I became vegetative, no job, nothing to do during the day. I lost my confidence, I didn't want to look for another job. I truly hated myself because I was ruining my wife and daughter's mood."

Rishi's hand trembled, his face turned ashen. Travis stood up and sat down next to Rishi. He put his hand over Rishi's trembling hand, ever so gently. He could hear Rishi's deep breathing. "It's okay, it's okay," said Travis.

"It's not okay," said Rishi, "It's not. I focused on the wrong things in life and forgot what was truly important. How I wish I had gathered myself, stopped myself, how I wish even at that stage, I'd stopped things from getting worse."

Travis stayed silent.

Rishi poured it all out. "I continued in that horrible mood until the wedding. At the grand wedding the thought that my wife's brothers paid for the wedding, hounded me. I felt like an outsider at my own daughter's wedding. And then I started drinking."

> *Family is the most important thing for many of us, yet we ignore and abuse our relationships to chase misguided external goals.*

Oh, no, thought Travis.

"I drank till I was drunk out of my mind. I didn't realize it, I verbally abused my wife, her brothers, and created a terrible, terrible scene. My wife was so upset and embarrassed," cried Rishi tears rolling down. "My daughter, I don't even know what she must have felt." Rishi wailed. Travis squeezed his hand.

"My high school friend whisked me away to my hotel room and put me to sleep. The only silver lining was that by God's grace none of my daughter's in-laws saw me out-of-control. I can't imagine if they had seen me like that. That would've really hurt my daughter's married life." Rishi held his head.

"I'm stunned," said Travis. "You're caring and considerate, how could you ruin your daughter's precious day."

Rishi cried out, trembling, "She came to me the day after the wedding and said, 'Daddy, I hate you!'" Rishi started crying. Travis put his arm around him to console him. "Oh, God, Oh, God, what did I do." Rishi sobbed uncontrollably.

"Have some water." Travis handed Rishi the glass of water. Rishi drank it all. "Let me fetch some more," said Travis. He got up and filled it up with cold water. Rishi drank some more. "Would you like more?" asked Travis.

"No, thanks."

Travis sat down on the couch on his side and waited for Rishi to compose himself.

"How are things now?"

Rishi looked away, needing some time. Travis reflected on how life affects people.

"Priya's fine, she's forgiven me." Rishi looked back at Travis, "She visited us a few months ago, she's happy."

"Good."

"I miss her so much. I really miss her."

"And, your wife?"

"She hasn't forgiven me. We live in the same house, but we're living as if we're separated."

"You'll aren't contemplating —"

"Divorce? No, never. We're quite traditional, Indian in our thinking. She'd never divorce me, and same here."

"Have you tried reconciling?"

"Umm…"

"You haven't?"

"Not… really," Rishi confessed, "after we returned to Houston we haven't really spoken to each other much. I find every excuse to travel. In the beginning, I'd come to Vegas or go to

Louisiana practically every other weekend, I'd gamble, drink, get an escape."

"Seriously?" Travis threw up his left arm. "After drinking got you into such a bind!"

"Yeah," said Rishi as he exhaled deeply. "I drank a lot for the first two, three months until I realized my life had completely disintegrated. Then I reminded myself I needed to go back to meditating and find solace in life. It hasn't been a straight recovery, I've gone back and forth. It's been tough, but meditation has stabilized me. I'm becoming much calmer and... dare I say happier."

"What about your wife?" asked Travis.

"What do you mean?"

"Calmer, happier?" said Travis.

"I wouldn't know." Rishi has a sheepish look.

Travis looked sternly. "How can you talk about helping mankind when you can't care enough about your own wife?"

"I do care about her. I care about her deeply."

"Well, what've you done for her? Let her suffer on her own."

"I did apologize to her when we came back to Houston. She hadn't talked to me in Mumbai after the wedding, and I thought maybe she would've cooled down."

"And?" asked Travis.

"Oh, no, she was full of anger, said some really nasty stuff." Rishi waved his hand.

"And, you?" said Travis.

"Well, I...." Rishi looked down.

"You gave it back too?" said Travis.

"I tried to be nice, but I was upset she'd taken money from her brothers and ruined the wedding."

"Rishi, are you listening to yourself, you talk about the mind and bringing it in control, and look at you man, your mind and your ego is out of control."

Rishi felt a little offended, he stared for a second and then eased. After a few deep breaths, he said, "Okay, yes, my ego was hurting. But now I know in the grand scheme of things it doesn't matter, my daughter's happiness is all that matters."

"Exactly, it was never about your ego. I'm not saying your wife was right in borrowing money, she should've been more sensitive to how strongly you felt. No wait, I'll side with her, her focus was on your daughter and her wedding day. She was right," said Travis.

"I guess it's water under the bridge," said Rishi. "Next week is our 25th wedding anniversary, don't know if we're spending it together."

"Risheeee! Why haven't you reconciled with your wife?"

Rishi did not answer.

"Why not?" pressed Travis.

"I began practicing meditation, became focused, got a new job and have been consumed with it, and —"

"You sure your ego's not stopping you?" pressed Travis.

"Well, it's not helping," said Rishi.

"Seriously, Rishi? You're going to go on living like that? You can't see how you're wife is suffering. She did nothing wrong, and you're punishing her."

"I'm not punishing her, I'm punishing myself."

"Rishi, wake up! Please. Don't let your ego stop you."

Rishi listened quietly.

"You need to find true bliss, and you're not going to find peace if you don't reconcile," said Travis turning counselor.

"I'll find bliss, I'm making progress," said Rishi.

"Fine, I know. But don't you think if you lifted that burden, you'll be happier and make faster progress towards peace. Wouldn't you want to move faster? Why let fear and ego come in the way? Progress Rishi, don't be stagnant. Let the river flow. Let the river flow!"

Rishi looked down at the floor. Then, he stood up, walked up the stairs to the bedroom and closed the door.

Travis rested his head back on the couch and closed his eyes. His mind raced feverishly. He was stunned and shocked by Rishi's revelations. He had always thought Rishi was well-off, so the money challenges were a surprise, but what Travis could not get over were Rishi's personal challenges. Rishi was a mentor, a person to look up to. Travis felt his ground had shaken. If Rishi could be so vulnerable then what could he expect from anyone else, including himself.

Travis took out his phone but put it back without checking his emails. He stood up and paced along the windows. He paused. It struck him, Rishi with all his knowledge and wisdom still needed to be watchful, not allow his mind and ego take control. Travis realized if Rishi needed to be careful, how much more he would need to be careful to manage his own mind. Travis took a deep breath. Then he turned to the windows and drew the curtains aside revealing a beautiful late afternoon sky scattered with clouds, not too bright. The sun played peekaboo through the clouds. He heard the door open upstairs and saw Rishi walk out of the bedroom.

Rishi walked down the stairs and came up to the window. His eyes were puffed up, but his face was calm. He looked out at the view. "I'm going to reconcile with Suchi. I'll do whatever it takes." Rishi looked at Travis. "I'll apologize sincerely for all the hurt I've created in her life, in our lives, and in our daughter's life. All the hurt because of my hungry mind. The Universe has blessed me by showing me the path to my happy soul. I'll not let my hungry mind ruin my family's happiness, and prevent the blissful union with my soul."

Travis took a step toward Rishi, shook his hand, and then embraced him in a tight hug, both deriving comfort and peace from the embrace.

A beam of sunray broke through the clouds and shone on Rishi's face. He stepped back from the embrace. Travis saw the light on Rishi's face. "Should I draw the curtains?" asked Travis.

"No, let's leave it open. It feels nice," said Rishi. "I need some water."

They refilled their glasses from the refrigerator. As they sat back down, Rishi said, "I've never understood how can I make huge mistakes in my life and yet be so driven to spirituality."

"Well...," said Travis.

"I can understand the desire to be spiritual," said Rishi, "but what I can't understand is the progress I make when I meditate. Spirituality is growing in me leaps and bounds, in spite of my huge ego, in spite of the hurt I've created, in spite of the sins I've committed."

"That's why you think spirituality is independent of deeds?" said Travis.

Rishi nodded.

"You should be happy about that," said Travis.

"Believe me, I am," said Rishi. "It has brought meaning to my life, stabilized me, otherwise, I would've spun out of control. Quieting my mind and meditation has saved me."

"You're very lucky," said Travis.

"Guess I'm lucky because I've found the spiritual path, or rather it has found me. I'm also unlucky because I'm aware of how the mind works. I can talk all I want about how the mind should stay in control, but I know how my own mind can break the banks and lead me through a horrifying ride. Knowing very well how I should've behaved better is painful."

Rishi looked down. "When I went upstairs, I fought with myself. I've become spiritual and yet my ego is so strong and alive. It's stronger than ever, it may have become a little dormant, but beneath the surface, it's still strong."

"It's strong in all of us," said Travis as he shook his head.

"If you hadn't challenged me I probably would've gone forever without reconciling with my wife. Knowing that I could've done that is so painful. How could I even think that way? ...This is hard, very hard."

In a supportive tone, Travis said, "Stop beating yourself up, not many people would've accepted their mistake and agree to put their ego down."

"I hope someday my spirituality will rise to the level where my mind becomes completely at peace and my ego sublimated," said Rishi.

"It'll happen, I know it will," said Travis.

"Thank you so much, Travis." Rishi touched his heart. "Would you please bless me, by touching me on the forehead?"

"Sure." Travis got up and came close. He touched the space between Rishi's eyes with his thumb.

Rishi closed his eyes. "Would you please put your palm on my eyes, and then touch the top of my head?"

Travis obliged. After a minute Rishi opened his eyes, looking calmer. He pressed his hands and bowed. "Thank you."

"Sure, buddy, any time."

"Do you want to stop?" asked Rishi.

"No, I want to finish our discussion."

"You sure?" asked Rishi.

"Yeah, I'm sure." Travis looking directly into Rishi's eyes. "I'm not much different from you on how close I am to the edge," said Travis. "I must seriously try spirituality — now — so I don't go off the deep end. I really must."

"You won't go off the deep end, I promise you won't."

Travis nodded. "Okay."

"I could use some fresh air," said Rishi. "May we sit out on the patio?"

"Sure," said Travis. Travis picked himself a bottle of apple juice, Rishi picked an orange. They sat under a big umbrella.

"Nice weather," said Travis.

"Luckily, it's still March," said Rishi. He looked up at the clouds. "This world is so painful when we're not at peace, and so beautiful when we're at peace."

Our lives are much bigger than the events in our life. Good and bad times, all pass. Smile! Smile all the time!

Every person on Earth faces challenges and problems at some point in their lives. Calming our minds is the only way to face life's challenges in the best manner.

Chapter 18: Meditation

Travis drank his apple juice.

Rishi sat quietly, almost meditatively.

Travis looked at Rishi. "Can you teach me meditation?"

"Of course, it's the best gift I can ever share. And, let me give credit where it's due. The ancient Indian sages discovered meditation thousands of years ago. It's their biggest gift to humanity. I sincerely thank them."

"I thank them too," said Travis. "Okay, so I know the part about sitting down, folded legs with your back erect, and closing your eyes."

"You can be comfortable, there isn't a need to be stiff. I use a pillow behind my back many times."

"Do I have to fold the legs?" asked Travis.

"I like to fold my legs, but you can sit in a chair. I like sitting on the bed, or the carpet, something comfortable. I simply put one leg over the other, not the difficult cross-legged, lotus pose."

"What about your hands?"

"Most of the time, I find my fingers are interlocked, or slightly overlaying each other. I don't worry much about the pose, I like to be comfortable."

"Got it," said Travis. "How to control the mind?"

"That's the trick, you don't. Wait, before we go on, I need to say this. There are many aids and techniques, meditative music, reciting muntruhs, focusing on certain objects, breathing exercises, and hand mudras or gestures. You can choose what you like. The technique I use is basic, doesn't use any aids. I don't even recite a muntruh," said Rishi.

"Don't people say Om when meditating?" asked Travis.

"I recite Om when I pray or I want to calm down, but not during meditation," said Rishi. "When I meditate, I sit down and let things happen."

"Why do people say Om?"

"Om is the primordial sound according to the ancient Indian sages. It represents the essence of the entire Universe. It has numerous meanings," said Rishi.

"Like?"

"First, Om represents the states of the mind — the waking state, the dream state, and the deep sleep state. And, it represents the fourth state, pure stillness, the meditative state, or as I call it the soul state. The soul state is the substratum, or foundation, or envelope, in which the other states exist."

"That's why they chant Om when meditating."

"Yes, there's another angle too," said Rishi. "When you say Om, you generate vibrations in your body. Om is made up of three sounds, aaa, uuu, mmm, and a fourth element. When you say aaa, it generates vibrations in your stomach, uuu generates vibrations in your throat, and mmm in your head. As you recite Om, the vibrations travel from your stomach to your throat and to your head. You are channeling your energy upwards when you recite Om."

"What is the fourth element?" said Travis.

"Silence. The wave of energy reaches the top and connects with the silent infinite. All the sounds of aaa, uuu, and mmm exist on the foundation of silence. Silence is always present. Any sound you hear is silence plus that sound."

Travis smiled a little in admiration of the point.

"Red colored water is red color plus water," said Rishi. "Green water is green color plus water. Colorless water is present always. Silence and the soul state are the colorless water, not seen or heard, but always present."

"Your explanation is awesome!" Travis put his hands on his chest. "So, why don't you say Om?"

Rishi smiled. "I do when I'm praying, but not so much when I am meditating. Maybe I should... but, at some point when you enter deep meditation, your recitations have to stop. As long as you recite and focus on it, your mind's still active. Om recitation is powerful in calming the mind, but at some point, you've to leave everything behind."

"Can I chant Om or a muntruh?" said Travis.

"Yes, sure, of course. For many people, chanting a muntruh, or reciting their God's name can have a powerful effect. It's like using an exercise machine. I prefer exercises which only use my body weight," said Rishi.

"You're the keep it simple, keep it natural, guy."

"Yeah, but we're all different and that's okay. You can choose what works for you." Then with a grin, Rishi said, "You can chant your wife's name if you like."

"Are you kidding me? That's not going to calm me down."

"Wait till I tell her," said Rishi as he laughed. So did Travis.

"My point is," said Rishi, "chant whatever appeals to you, whatever calms your mind down."

"I will," said Travis. "I think I need an aid."

"Use any technique you find useful. I've been meditating for years and never used any aids. I don't want to use a crutch or training wheels if you will, because ultimately you've to let them go. It may take me longer, but I want my mind to calm down naturally, I don't try to control it."

"Doesn't your mind run around?" asked Travis.

"It does, but to me that's okay. Sometimes my mind runs around for the entire time I sit in meditation. What that means is my mind had so many thoughts it needed to process. I don't short-circuit that. I like to let my mind process and clean up everything it has going. When it's done, it becomes calm. I just wait for it. That's my simple meditation technique."

"It's similar to the analogy of a puppy," said Travis. "If a puppy is energetic, you let it run around and use up all its energy. Then it'll automatically come sit at your feet."

"Exactly right. If we constrain the puppy before he's exhausted his energy, he'll still be anxious and difficult to control. But once he's had sufficient time to run around, he automatically becomes docile. The mind's exactly the same."

"Just let the mind be." Travis looked at the sky and felt the gentle breeze caress his face.

Rishi floated his hand. "Meditation is like floating."

"How so?" asked Travis looking back at Rishi.

"You cannot say I'm floating. That's nonsensical."

"Why?" asked Travis.

"You can say I'm doing nothing, lying relaxed in the water, and floating is happening naturally," said Rishi.

"Okay," said Travis.

"Same with meditation. You can say my mind's doing nothing, and meditation is happening naturally. You just have to practice doing nothing. Meditation is not something you do. Meditation is something that happens to you."

"I've tried to meditate before. I sit down but my mind doesn't calm down," said Travis. "It keeps thinking of things and then either I'm out of time or I get restless enough to stop."

"Remember, meditate without expectations," said Rishi. "Do not judge your progress or lack of it. Don't look for results. Don't tell yourself, I feel calmer than yesterday or last week. Stop the focus on the outcome, focus on the effort. If you sit down for meditation and your mind doesn't calm down, don't despair, don't lament. In fact, don't give it any thought. The next day, sit down again and meditate. Let it take ten years if it has to. One day your mind will slow down. Just do it."

> *Meditation is not something you do. Meditation is something that happens to you.*

"Like jogging, just got to do it," said Travis.

"Yeah, just keep doing it. Unbeknownst to you, every time you meditate, regardless of the quality of the session at the surface, your subconscious is changing. Your mind might tell you, I'm not making progress, meditation isn't making any difference, I still feel miserable, but don't let that stop you. What your conscious mind thinks has little impact on your spiritual progress. Every time you meditate, it leaves an impression deep down. Don't think, just meditate."

"Okay...," Travis smiled, "maybe, it'll grow on me."

Rishi touched his thumb and index finger. "Sometimes my meditation is so good, all my consternation stops... I experience complete stillness. Most of the time, the meditation session doesn't go all the way, but so what. When I'm dealing with the material world, I'm at the boiling point. If I can take down my temperature even a few degrees, I've made progress, and most importantly I feel instant relief."

"That makes sense," said Travis.

"Of course, whether you're able to cool down depends on how much latent heat you've accumulated. Every day we engage with the world we add latent energy. That's why we must be careful with addictions, they raise our temperature the most."

"Got it," said Travis.

Rishi was about to speak, when Travis said, "What if sitting down gets boring?"

"Yeah, sitting down can be boring," said Rishi, "but if you make it a habit it'll become easier."

"If I make it a habit, then what?" said Travis.

"Then your mind will begin to calm down. Sometimes toward the end of the session, sometimes during the session before it runs around more. The mind will eventually learn to quiet down and become calm."

"Then what?" said Travis.

"Then you'll see God!" said Rishi as he roared out laughing.

"Excuse me!"

"Okay, okay," said Rishi raising his palms to pacify Travis. "When the mind is quiet, you'll become the observer, you'll become aware of the gaps between your thoughts, you'll become aware of the silence, the sweet silence."

"Is that the soul? Is that nirvana?"

"No, nirvana takes longer. As you experience silence, greater happiness and peace will fill you. Your mind won't be as agitated. The next time you meditate, your mind will calm down faster. This cycle will feed on itself if you're consistent."

"What if you break the cycle?" asked Travis.

"No different than the gym. If you take a break, you have to work back up. The longer the break, the longer it takes to get back to previous levels."

"Any benefits from previous efforts?" asked Travis.

"Yes, of course, it helps. The residue or remnants are always there, so it's not as hard as the very first time you started, but the duration of the break does have an impact," said Rishi.

"Do some people make faster progress than others?" asked Travis.

"Uh, I better be careful," said Rishi.

"What do you mean?"

"When you compare your meditation effort with others, you undermine your progress. Meditation's not a worldly pursuit, you don't ever want to compare notes on your progress because eventually, you'll entertain thoughts about either how well you're doing or not. Either of those thoughts will ruin your ability to meditate. Don't share, don't compare. Don't compete with others. Don't compete with yourself. Just meditate."

"Okay, I won't compete," said Travis.

"Having said that, every person is different. Some will make faster progress than others will. It has to do with many factors. Don't think about it," said Rishi. "Sit down for meditation with yourself and not bring anyone else into your meditation."

"This is a solo activity."

"Yes. Keep your mind free of other people. It's ironic."

"What?" asked Travis.

"Being lonely is horrible, being alone is wonderful," said Rishi. "We need to learn to be alone, and learn to cherish our own selves."

"Don't be lonely, be alone," repeated Travis.

"You have to let go. Don't hold on to your thoughts. Watch them as an observer. Like a kid standing at the edge of the park and watching all the proceedings. Just watch."

> *Do not be lonely, be alone. Spend time with your own self.*

"Okay."

"Then surrender yourself," said Rishi.

"Surrender?" asked Travis.

"Yes, stop thinking about Travis. Let Travis dissolve. In fact, a better word than surrender is sublimate."

"Sublimate is to... you told me before," said Travis.

"Sublimate it to become nobler, actually purer is a better description. It's dissolving, like sugar dissolves in water and becomes one with water. Your mind sublimates to become one with your soul, your core/fundamental essence. The identification with the ego, the persona Travis is gone, you're just your base profound energy, the soul within you."

"Melt away the ego," said Travis as he smiled.

"Yes, melting away the layers that prevent us from experiencing the soul. And, also melting as in ice melting into water. Ice is hard and has a rigid structure. Water is soft and nimble. When we strip away the hard ego, the stubbornness of our memories and personalities, we're left in the presence of the soul, which is soft and placid."

"Wow," said Travis.

"Yeah. Like anything in life, we gravitate to things we've done a lot," said Rishi. "The more exercise you do, the more it becomes a part of you, and the more you miss it."

"Same applies to spiritual practice?" asked Travis.

"Yes, the more you do it, the richer the experiences, and the more you'd want to do it. The more peaceful you are, the richer the meditation. Therefore it's important to do the slowing of the mind exercises we discussed earlier," said Rishi.

"Hoping all my stress melts away as I meditate."

"We can tell our conscious mind, don't be anxious, but the subconscious mind won't listen, it remains anxious."

"True," said Travis.

"When you quiet the conscious mind, the subconscious mind automatically processes its fears, lowering anxiety."

"Stress and anxiety must be embedded deep," said Travis.

"Yes, they are. When we live with anxiety, fear, and greed for long periods, we become selfish, irate, and meaner. Meditation changes our nature and makes us nicer beings."

"I certainly need… to be nicer," said Travis.

"You will be. Another key phenomenon will happen."

"What?" said Travis.

"As you experience quietude consistently, and have been doing it for some time, you'll find some things happening."

"What things?"

"You could be in a meeting, or driving, or waiting in a pizza line, and suddenly a wave of peace will fill you."

"Just like that, anywhere?" said Travis smiling like a toddler who had a sneak peek at a candy.

"Yeah, it's involuntary," said Rishi. "It'll just happen. The inner quietude pervades you even when you're consumed with daily activities, as if it's a reminder to you of its presence."

"That's cool," said Travis.

"Yes, it is! We'll be in automatic meditation mode even though we're not sitting down for meditation. We could be in the middle of a loud concert with thousands of people and still feel the blissful silence within us. It's the most amazing thing."

"I'm getting goosebumps," said Travis.

"Me too," said Rishi caressing his left arm. "Meditation is the key to enter the spiritual dimension. We can come back to the material world and then transcend back into the spiritual realm. Of course, once you've been exposed to the spiritual dimension, the material world loses its hold on you. You don't take it as seriously as you did before. You acknowledge it, but you see it for what it is, a movie playing on the screen, which will end." Rishi touched his shirt. "You watch the movie, but if it's raining in the movie you never check if your clothes are wet. You never forget the movie rain is an illusion."

"And, that is self-realization?"

"Being completely dissolved in the spiritual realm, becoming one with our soul is self-realization!" Rishi glided his hand. "It's the ultimate yog, the ultimate union. It's the way we connect with the infinite! Connect with God!"

Travis bowed his head with palms touching. So did Rishi.

"I'm curious, when did you first meditate? How did it start for you?" asked Travis. "Did you practice —"

"I'll tell you all of it, but, first, may we move back inside?" Rishi pushed his chair back. "These patio chairs aren't the most comfortable."

"No problem," said Travis. They moved in.

Meditation is the antidote to our problems in the short-term and the key to Ultimate Happiness in the long-term.

Meditate every day, like there is no tomorrow. And, meditate without expectations, meditate just for the sake of meditating.

Chapter 19: Path Forward

Rishi sat back down on the plush sofa. "Much better."

Travis settled in. "So when did you first meditate?"

Rishi smiled. "Long story, starts in my childhood."

"Love to hear it," said Travis.

"My father was a devout follower of a swami," said Rishi. "My mother would sing devotional songs as she did her chores. I can still feel the feelings of bliss and peace from her songs."

"Sounds wonderful. You sure had a religious family."

"It was more spiritual. As Hindus, we followed the traditions. My Dad, however, would search the philosophical questions, who am I, why I am here. I enjoyed listening to his discussion with his friends. I would watch my Dad meditate often, completely lost in meditation. As a family, we'd go to the large public spiritual discourses of tens of thousands of people. When I was young the discourses were difficult to understand, but as I entered my teens, it began to make sense."

"Okay," said Travis.

"I started meditating on my own," said Rishi. "My Father didn't push me to do it. I guess my Mom and Dad had created the right environment. I must've been only fifteen, in one of my meditation sessions, I had a deep meditative experience."

"Just fifteen!" said Travis.

"Yeah," said Rishi. "Time went by in a mere blink of an eye. When I got up, I was in a trance, as if the whole world had become peaceful, surreal. I left the room and joined my family for dinner. I didn't share what had happened. I felt as if I was floating. I knew then that whatever the gurus were talking about was real. I remember that incident as one of my strongest meditative experiences."

"I know I'm not supposed to compare," said Travis, "but can you describe in detail what you experience in meditation? Please."

Rishi replied, "When I sit for meditation, and my mind is completely still, I experience stillness and peace, which leads to pure bliss. When my mind is silent, so are its worldly addictions. At that moment, I'm completely free, it's the most beautiful thing on this Earth."

"Wow," said Travis.

"That feeling, that experience is more sweet, more... I don't even have a word to describe it, more everything than anything else in this world. More than my first job offer, more than the first time I fell in love, more than the day of my marriage, more than the first time I held my newborn daughter in my arm, and I promise you that was really, really cool."

"You're kidding me," said Travis.

"No, this blissful experience is indescribable and it takes me in its arm like nothing else does. If only... all I want is to be lost in that experience. It's the truest of all experiences," said Rishi.

Rishi closed his eyes, slumping back into the sofa. Talking about the experience had made the experience come alive for him. He let himself be still and became completely peaceful.

Travis saw a faint, sweet smile on Rishi's face with his head tilted upward just a little. He looked blissful.

Travis thought about how things come together in life, how he had met Rishi after five years, and how the discussion had become so deep. He remembered his son Nathan, however, it did not seem to cause as much pain as the day before.

Rishi slowly opened his eyes. He smiled gently, like an author who had written another important chapter in his book. Travis smiled too feeling the gentle bliss emanating from Rishi.

"Sorry, I was lost," said Rishi.

Travis nodded to indicate it was all right. He could tell Rishi was still in the moment even though his eyes were open. Rishi smiled and gestured inviting Travis to resume.

"This blissful experience... it's different than the other wonderful moments of your life?" asked Travis.

Rishi picked up his glass of water and after taking a sip, said, "Those were ecstatic moments. I remember when I received my first job offer, it was for thirty-five thousand, as a poor student that was a king's ransom to me. I felt I was in heaven, as if my feet were not on the ground. An incredible moment of joy."

"I felt the same when I landed my first investment," said Travis. "I couldn't stop thanking my angel investor."

"Nice. I felt the same when I saw Suchi the first time. I fell in love at first sight," said Rishi. "I can still remember the tingling I felt when I'd be with her in those days."

Travis smiled. "How romantic!"

"That feeling and the feeling when Priya was born, they're all out-of-this-world feelings. Incredible joyous moments, incredibly beautiful moments."

"So, how are they different from the bliss you experience?"

"Those moments had joy and excitement, huge spurts of energy, I wanted to dance in the streets, dance on rooftops, dance holding hands, just an expression of love and delight at the world, and wonderful emotions in my heart," said Rishi.

Travis smiled.

"The bliss I experience is not energy, it's not excitement. It's contentment, it is peace, I do not grin and dance, I smile and smile. I feel as if I am on a high, I feel as if the entire world is such a beautiful place. It feels deep and internal. Unlike the moments of joy in my life, my mind's not racing, I don't feel as if I need to do anything. I just want to be suspended in air, free-floating, no desire compelling me to do anything. Completely without worries, completely without judgment, no desires, no wants, no needs for anything or anyone. Just chill. That's right." Rishi smiled. "Just chill. As if you're on the most beautiful beach and you're completely happy with yourself."

"I wanna be on that beach!" said Travis.

"I kid you not," said Rishi, "it's a beautiful experience."

"What's the problem then," asked Travis, "why aren't you in that state all the time, why do you talk about —"

"My shortcomings and struggles?" said Rishi.

"Yeah, you know how to get there, why not stay there?"

"Wish I could. I'm still figuring it out," said Rishi. "You can be blissful, but eventually, at least for me, it wears out, and you return to this world and you have things to attend to."

"So, should you go to the Himalayas?" asked Travis.

"Well, no. I return to this world because I've things to do and because I want to. I can't imagine being in the Himalayas all the time. My mind needs engagement, I can't just cut myself from the world. That's the push-pull between spirituality and the world. And, frankly, I'm trying to figure out how to weave them together. I truly believe you can be spiritual while engaging in this world, fulfilling your obligations to your family, friends, and to your own self," said Rishi. "I hope I'm not wrong."

"You want to have your cake and eat it too," said Travis.

Rishi smiled. "I believe it can be done. If I meditate regularly, the experience will become richer, last longer and there will come a time when I'll be fixed in the blissful state, it'll never wear off. I don't know how many years of regular meditation it might take, but I'm certain that is where this leads."

"The path to nirvana," said Travis.

"All signs point to it," replied Rishi. "If you read the experiences of the ancient sages, they all describe it. That is what the ancient Indian sages described as self-realization and Buddha describes as nirvana. The point where your experience of the soul is so strong, you're in permanent and endless bliss."

"I don't mean to be skeptical," said Travis, "you're so sure about the path of meditation and how it leads to ultimate and infinite happiness. You aren't there yet, how can you be so sure you'll be able to achieve it?"

"I can feel it. I can feel it coming. Just like someone who goes to the gym and see his muscles develop, he or she knows they're on the right path and if they persist they'll develop a well-toned, highly muscular body," said Rishi.

"Gotta to be persistent," said Travis.

"Yes. I wish I could become truly persistent and overcome the hang-ups in my mind. If I break free from my hungry mind, I'll be on the journey of my life."

"My good wishes are with you," said Travis.

"Thank you, thank you. I need your blessings and good wishes, please pray for me," said Rishi pressing his hands together and bowing his head slightly.

"Absolutely, and please pray for me too," said Travis.

Rishi nodded. "I will. As you experience spirituality, your mind moves away naturally from the temptations — I should use the word distractions. When I meditate regularly, my urges become lesser. That's why I'm not too worried about my deeds, as long as I meditate regularly, my so-called temptations will evaporate away. It affects every aspect of life including my deepest urge to make money. It doesn't hound me as much. I know I still need to make money and go to work, but I'm not on the edge. I trade stocks in a better frame of mind, my fear is lesser and I make fewer bad decisions."

"So spirituality distracts you from the distractions." Travis smiled.

Rishi smiled. "Interestingly said." Rishi tapped his forehead. "Many scriptures talk about controlling the mind. They say control the senses so you don't get caught in the material world. But that's an awfully difficult thing to do."

"No kidding," said Travis.

"The mind can't be controlled," said Rishi, "but it can be redirected, until the time you train it to be quiet."

"I know all about redirection. I used to play video games non-stop and my parents yelling at me made no difference. Then they devised the idea of getting me involved in basketball. It changed my life, made me focus," said Travis.

"I didn't know that," said Rishi.

"Yup, I played basketball through college and then got interested in computers. Rest is history," said Travis.

"My biggest regret in life… my biggest regret is I didn't meditate every day," said Rishi. "If I had, my life would be entirely different… it would've been a million times richer. I would've enjoyed every moment in life, enjoyed life with my family, instead of living in a frenzied rat-race." Rishi sighed.

"Isn't that really sad, you're describing my condition," said Travis.

"I've eaten dinner with my family practically every day of my life, and yet I wasn't there," said Rishi. "There physically but not mentally… and for what… I feel I've missed out on my entire life. I miss my family. Now life has slipped past me."

"That's not true," said Travis. "You have the entirety of the rest of your life in front of you. Even if you're going to live for only one more day, you must be enthusiastic about it, life hasn't slipped you by. Every day is precious. Ask me! I'd do anything, anything to get one more day with Nathan."

Rishi lowered his eyes, slightly ashamed. "You're right, I should practice what I preach and stop complaining. I need to stop living in the troubles of my past, and look forward to making every day worthwhile."

"You know that already," said Travis, "there's something not working for you?"

"You're very perceptive… my challenge… is not that I don't know how to transcend the spiritual and the worldly matters. My challenge is the lack of discipline. I need to meditate regularly, and that's my biggest fear for you too, will you be regular."

"Why aren't you regular? Too much work?" asked Travis.

"Yeah, I'm busy… but… sometimes I don't feel like meditating," admitted Rishi.

"Really?" Travis had a surprised look.

"Believe it or not," said Rishi nodding his head, partially disappointed with himself. "I preach meditation to everyone I meet, friends, colleagues, the bartender. And, yet, I don't do it."

"You mean do it regularly," said Travis.

"Yes," said Rishi, feeling a huge weight on himself.

"Why… why don't you?"

Rishi shook his head. "Sometimes I just don't feel like it. I'm happy, and I feel I don't need it. There are days when I'm plain lazy, it feels like a chore. I rather wake up in the morning and not meditate. I rather read the news or watch TV."

"That's okay. Is that so bad?" said Travis.

"Well, once I break the pattern, I go many days without meditating, sometimes weeks and months," said Rishi. "That's when things begin to break down. Soon, I get irritable —"

"You struggle."

"I do, and it's difficult," said Rishi. "Then I've to bring myself back to the regiment and start meditating regularly. After a few days, I begin to calm down and feel better again."

"It's a seesaw." Travis moved his hand back and forth.

"Yeah. Meditation always gives, but I've to show up to receive," said Rishi, reminding himself he must stay consistent.

"How can you be more disciplined?" said Travis.

"That's the million dollar question. Look at me, I should exercise more," said Rishi. "I know that but I don't, at least not often enough."

"You look fine," said Travis.

"I need to do more, then I'll look as fit as you."

"That's not going to happen." Travis smiled. "Thought you said meditation is enticing. It'll pull you in."

"Yes, it does, and it becomes richer as you do it regularly and continuously. But any cycle can be broken. And, that's been my challenge. That's why I like talking to anyone I can find about all of this, it puts me in the mood and reminds me."

Rishi paused to reaffirm his resolve. He closed his eyes and felt the vibrations in his body he always felt after good meditation sessions. "Thank you... Travis, thank you for allowing me to talk to you about spirituality, thank you for listening to me, and thank you for pointing out things that are so obvious and yet I ignore them."

"You're welcome, but, you're the one who's helping me."

"We're helping each other. I need someone to talk to. I need to do this every day, so I can be reminded," said Rishi.

"Ah, you need a gym-buddy," said Travis, pleased with his suggestion.

"You're right, I do," smiled Rishi. "Will you be my gym-buddy?"

Travis hesitated.

"I know, you're in California," said Rishi.

"Well, maybe you need to form a group in Houston of like-minded people," said Travis.

"Yeah, there's even a Sanskrit word for it — suthsung," said Rishi. "Suthsung has two parts, suth, pronounced s-uh-th, and sung, pronounced just like the word sung. Suth means good or truth, sung means company."

"Maybe I should start a suthsung in San Jose," said Travis.

"Well, I'm sure there are many groups already existing."

"But they'll have their own beliefs," said Travis.

"That's true," said Rishi nodding.

"Need a group of meditators who don't talk too much."

"Sorry with all the talking," said Rishi.

"I didn't mean you," said Travis with a chastising look.

"I know. Which is the same hesitancy I have, I don't want to sit and debate ad nauseam about religion and philosophy. I want to interface with people who are calm and help each other progress towards quietude. It's difficult to find people who aren't going to force their religious beliefs on you, who are simple, sincere, and interested in true spiritual progress," said Rishi.

"I know what you mean, people who are open, not too rigid," said Travis.

Rishi leaned forward. "People like you. Every discussion of ours has left me with a greater sense of peace."

"Maybe we should talk often on the phone," said Travis.

"Please, I'd like that. Can you find the time?" said Rishi.

"Going to make it a priority. I'll schedule a call every week," said Travis.

"A man of action," said Rishi.

"If you don't put it on the schedule, won't happen," said Travis.

"Will you put your meditation on the schedule too?" asked Rishi.

"Yup. Are you?" said Travis.

"Man, you're tough," said Rishi. "I definitely will, though I want to get to the point where I'm in a meditative mode all day, regardless of whether I'm at work, in a meeting, or at home on the weekend."

"You can do it if you put your mind to it… oops, if you take your mind out of it," said Travis as he smiled.

Rishi smiled too. "Yes, I can." He felt enthused and excited about the future, a feeling of security, knowing he had a soul with whom he could share his deepest thoughts, and get due understanding, consideration, and encouragement.

"A peaceful mind," said Rishi, "transmits positive energy to the people around, and to the Universe as a whole. As more of people find peace within, the world around us will change."

"There needs to be a meditation revolution," said Travis.

Rishi looked at Travis curiously, his eyes twinkling.

"Where everyone on Earth meditates, from kids to senior citizens," said Travis.

Rishi closed his eyes. "If a majority of the people meditate and find peace, Earth will indeed become heaven."

"Meditate, meditate, meditate regularly," said Travis and recited the spiritual muntruh, "Quiet my hungry mind, let my happy soul shine."

Rishi touched his heart and smiled. "Meditate, meditate, meditate. An undertaking that can transform the world. Do you remember the steps of the spiritual path?"

Meditate, meditate, meditate!!!

"Yes, transform our thoughts, mature our perspectives, quiet our mind, and our soul will reveal itself," said Travis.

"And, through our soul, we shall connect with the infinite Himself," said Rishi.

"You had promised to show me God in his full glory," said Travis. "You haven't forgotten have you?"

Just learn to be. Do not think... just be!

Rishi laughed. "No, I haven't. I do have something for you that is — mind expanding. It's huger than huuuuge."

*If majority of the people meditate and
experience internal peace,
Earth will indeed become heaven.*

Meditate! Meditate! Meditate!

*Quiet Your Hungry Mind,
Let Your Happy Soul Shine!*

Chapter 20: God, Universe, and Man

"Why is God so elusive?" asked Travis. "Connecting through our souls is fine, but shouldn't it be easier, we should be able to go somewhere and shake hands with Him."

"Let me share something funny," said Rishi. "Time magazine ran a cover many years ago, 'Is God Dead?'"

"Did they really?" said Travis as he smiled.

"Yeah, it's like you asking why's God not easy to find," said Rishi. "What do you think? Could He die or be dead?"

Travis shrugged. "You tell me."

"No, God is not dead!" Rishi looked down from the edge of his spectacles and waved his hand. "God cannot die!" He followed in a heavy, declarative tone. "God is neither born nor can he die. God exists. Just exists. Always!"

"Do you really know if God can't die?" asked Travis playing his role of a good student of philosophy.

Rishi smiled. "By definition, whatever the concept God is, it can't die, if it could die then it's not God."

It took a moment for Travis to digest that. He wanted to follow up, then realized it is a conjecture anyway, so he did not.

Recognizing Travis's reticence, Rishi said, "God's been described as omnipresent, omniscient, omnipotent. God's been present all the time. Nothing can create or destroy God. God is all infinite in the dimensions of space, time, energy, and power, and the subtler dimensions we can't perceive," Rishi touched his forehead, "the dimensions beyond our senses."

"Know all of that, you got something new?" said Travis.

"Okayyyy… let me tell you something that might stop you in your tracks." Rishi smiled teasingly.

"What? Stop building it up. Is this the God in His full glory discussion you promised me?"

Rishi smiled. "Yeah!" Rishi took a deep breath, readying himself as an acrobat on stage about to perform his most elaborate, gravity-defying act. He held his index finger up high pointing to the skies, and then declared with a grand voice, "God is the Universe. The Universe is God."

> *God is the Universe.*
>
> *The Universe is God.*

"Excuse me!" said Travis more amazed than shocked.

"Yes." Rishi's voice had great purpose. "When I was young, I read in the Bhugvud Geet, Lord Krishun describes Himself, Him being God, as having no beginning, no middle, and no end. He adds God is neither born, nor dies, does not age, and cannot be destroyed. God is infinite in time and space."

"Okay."

"When I first read that description I was struck by the grandness and even audacity of the statement," said Rishi. "It was awe-inspiring and scary, difficult to comprehend."

"I can see that," said Travis.

"Then in school, I learned the attributes of the Universe. Infinite in space, no beginning, no middle, no end. The Universe has always existed and will always exist. I was bewildered. Two concepts, described in exactly the same manner. Lord

Krishun described God several thousand years ago, and science described the Universe only in the last hundred years or so." Rishi touched the tips of his finger and thumb. "It's astounding, how these two definitions overlay perfectly."

"Don't they say God created the Universe? So how can they be the same?" asked Travis.

"I know they say that," said Rishi. "But to me, the fact that the Universe and God have exactly the same qualities is too heavy to ignore. The only two things I know that are truly infinite — are God and the Universe. They must be the same!"

"Maaan," Travis shook his head, "hard for me to buy."

"I know," said Rishi, "because we've always thought of God as the creator. The question is if God created the Universe, then who created God?"

"That's crazy," said Travis as he raised his eyebrows, "who can create God? If God exists, He must've always existed."

Rishi smiled.

Travis frowned. "Now, you'll say whatever God is, it is included in your definition of the Universe, and hence the Universe exists forever."

Rishi grinned.

"Look at you grinning away, all smug," said Travis.

"I haven't even said anything," said Rishi, still grinning. "You made your own point."

"No, I made your point," said Travis.

"Yes, and thank you!" said Rishi. "Whatever is forever, whatever is permanent, and the foundation of all existence is God to you and the Universe to me."

"You've switched the hierarchy," said Travis. "Instead of God creating the Universe, you've made God a component of the Universe."

"No, I haven't," said Rishi. "I'm not distinguishing between God and the Universe. They are the same thing."

"How can they be the same thing?" said Travis. "Physicists say the universe is expanding. Is God expanding? The universe got created from the Big Bang."

Rishi shook his head. "Physicists must be language challenged." Rishi laughed but Travis barely smiled. Rishi said, "What they mean to say is the visible universe is expanding. Something that's infinite cannot expand. It'd be more accurate to say galaxies are moving away from each other. If the fish in one part of the ocean are swimming away from each other, doesn't mean the ocean is expanding. Physicists can't see the ends of the universe, it's infinite! To say the infinite is expanding is absurd. It's as misleading as saying the Earth is flat."

"I'll agree with that," said Travis, "infinite can't expand."

"The Universe was here before the Big Bang, and will always be here. Whether the matter in the visible-to-us-universe was squeezed in an infinitely small space or distributed all over space, doesn't matter, it's still part of the Universe. Big Bang is a matter-related event that happened in space. Space cannot be created or destroyed. It just exists! The Universe cannot be created or destroyed. God cannot be created or destroyed."

"Boy, this is heavy philosophy. I'll get a headache."

"No. you won't, stay with me," said Rishi. "It's quite incredibly beautiful and amazing when you think about it."

"Okay...." Travis put his fist to his mouth.

"When I use the word Universe I'm not limiting it to matter, the visible two trillion galaxies."

"Didn't they upgrade that number?" said Travis.

"Yes, they did," said Rishi. "Physicists used to say we have two hundred billion galaxies, and recently they said the number was ten times larger, and whoosh," Rishi waved his hand in the air, "they scaled up the universe."

"I'm sure they'll revise again," said Travis.

"I bet they will as the telescopes see further away," said Rishi. "The Universe has countless dimensions. The matter in the Universe is just one aspect of the Universe. All the scientifically proven visible and invisible energies such as x-rays and electromagnetic fields are another aspect."

"Okay," said Travis.

"Then you have what people call the supernatural aspects such as telepathy and psychic abilities. Not to mention, our own emotional energies. And, the one we've been talking about, our spiritual energy. Now, if you take all these dimensions, and I'm sure there are dimensions of the Universe that mankind has not discovered or understood or will ever understand —"

"We haven't scratched the surface," said Travis.

"If you take all these dimensions, known and unknown to man, and describe that as the Universe, Universe with a capital-U, in all its glory, then you're now describing God," said Rishi.

"Do you think the Universe itself is spiritual?" asked Travis with a twinkle in his eyes.

"Just like all energy is connected to each other, the souls of all the living things are connected and are part of the collective supreme soul, which is a part of the Universe, and that's what I call the spiritual dimension or maybe we should call it the spirit-dimension of the Universe."

"All right," said Travis.

"That's not all, the laws of the Universe, they're another dimension. The movement of galaxies may change, stars and planets may be born and die, but the laws of Physics aren't changing. Numbers change, but the laws of Mathematics remain the same." Rishi took a quick sip of water. "Species come and go, but biological laws remain the same. Every species, plant, animal, and even the smallest microorganism, wants to propagate and thrive. Biologically if not consciously, isn't that downright amazing?"

"Yup, it is," said Travis. "All life wants to thrive."

Gathering up steam, Rishi's voice boomed, "Even though atoms are separated by billions of light years, are not in contact with each other, yet they abide by the same physical and chemical laws. That's so beautiful and astounding. The laws of Physics, Chemistry, Biology, and Mathematics are omnipresent and omnipotent. The laws do not change. They're fundamental to existence, and are eternal."

Enthralled by the discussion, Rishi took a few breaths to slow himself and to calm his energy.

Reciting recent scientific postulations, Travis asked, "In a multiverse, universes are created and destroyed. Plus, the other universes may have different laws."

"The laws may be different, but the existence of laws is the unchanging part," said Rishi. "When I use the capital-U Universe, I include all the possible parallel universes and multiverses that might exist. I am referring to the Universe in its infinite extents and dimensions. All existence!"

Rishi raised his finger. "Actually it's all of existence and all of nothingness. When you remove all existence, you're left with nothingness. Nothingness is the ocean in which the waves of existence exists."

"Your capital-U Universe includes existence and nothingness?" asked Travis.

"Yes, the changing aspects of the Universe is dependent on the unchanging aspects. The waves in the ocean change, rising and falling, but the ocean is the changeless foundation."

Travis asked, "Little-u parallel universes may form and dissolve, but they're all part of your capital-U Universe?"

"Yes. Rain clouds form and dissipate, but the atmosphere is the changeless foundation. If we understand the changeless and the changing aspects, we'll see the cosmic dance of the Universe, the dance of God," said Rishi as he swayed his hands, lost in his explanation and enjoying the discussion every bit.

"Ooh, the dance of God," Travis smiled.

"The incredible dance of God!" said Rishi. "One may see the wave and the ocean as two distinct instances, but they're the same. The changing existence is like the wave, and the unchanging nothingness is like the ocean. God is everything, the momentary wave and the permanent ocean. God is all encompassing. The Universe is all-encompassing. God is the Universe! The Universe is God!"

Travis closed his eyes. "Wow! Thinking about God as the Universe... for the first time, I'm able to wrap my mind around the concept of God, if it ever is possible to wrap your mind around God."

"It's not," said Rishi. "Our minds can't do that, it can only get a tiny glimpse of the glory of God. That said, when I think about the Universe and its vastness, I feel closer to God."

Travis didn't say anything, letting it sink in. Rishi also became quiet and closed his eyes.

Travis watched in awe as he always did, amused by the peace on Rishi's face, but also beginning to glimpse the vastness, the profoundness of the philosophy.

"You said we can feel God only through the soul," said Travis. Now, you're describing the Universe as God itself. That means I can see God with my mind. Can I?"

Rishi smiled at Travis's logical deduction. "Very good, great question. It's true, once we realize God is the Universe, our minds can comprehend God a little easier. But our mind is still not the equipment to experience God in His magnificent glory. It's still like trying to taste the pizza with our eyes."

"But… why?" asked Travis.

"Our mind can't comprehend infinity. To feel a connection with every atom in the Universe, to be one with all the energy in the Universe, to connect with infinity itself, we must dive inwards and connect with our soul. The day we feel our soul, the day our soul shines through is the day we'll truly connect with, feel and experience this most amazing Universe in all its infinite glory. Meditation practitioners who experience the deepest meditation have described the feeling of infinity, no boundaries. They lose all sense of space, time, and their own personal identity. It's a feeling that encompasses all."

Rishi closed his eyes to experience the stillness in the Universe and in his own heart. After a few moments, Rishi opened his eyes. "I took a quick dip into my being," said Rishi.

Travis acknowledged him with a smile.

"You said, you pray to God," said Travis. "So, are you praying to the Universe and does it listen?"

"Oh, yes. The Universe is living energy and it responds."

"Actually, that's true," said Travis. "So many times, I hear people say, 'The Universe is sending me signals.' I say that too."

"You were looking to speak to someone," said Rishi. "I was looking to discuss spirituality with someone, and guess what, both our requests were answered."

"Yup, that's true," said Travis. "I loved what you have shared about God and Universe. I wonder when people will understand what is God."

"Human beings have trivialized God," said Rishi.

"I'll give you that," said Travis.

"We all say 'my God,' as if it's an object of our possession or an exclusive relationship. We want to feel we're better than others. My God is better than yours! My religion's better than yours, my scriptures are better than yours," said Rishi.

"Plain competitiveness," said Travis as he shrugged. "No one's understood what God is."

"That's why I really like the notion of the Universe in its full glory as God. Then I can't say my Universe, because that doesn't make sense, it's not my Universe, I'm a part of the Universe," said Rishi.

"You're part of the Universe. I'm part of it, so is everyone," said Travis.

> *God is much greater than man's limited thinking. Man's mind is incapable of comprehending God. Only man's soul is the handshake with God.*

"Now you're talking my friend," said Rishi. "I'm a part of this Universe and so are you, there's no notion of my Universe being better than yours. We're all the same because we're a part of the same, a common oneness. It doesn't matter what language you speak, what color your skin is, what gender you are, in fact, even what species you are, we're all a part of this Universe." Rishi interlocked his fingers. "Our divisions melt away, and now we can truly be in the pursuit of God, without the labels and names we have put on God becoming a hindrance or a distraction."

"Love that," said Travis. "We don't have to fight about God. The Universe is ours! This is utterly, bodaciously, mindboggling!" Travis jumped up for a high-five. Rishi did too.

Sitting back down, Rishi said, "It is mind-boggling and has incredible ramifications. Mankind has fought wars, killed people in the name of religion. All of that stupidity and narrowmindedness can stop now. No one can judge anyone else. No one can say you do not belong. There's no exclusion. Nature includes all of us. We're all part of the Universe."

We are the Universe. The Universe is us.

"No one can be denied," said Travis.

Rishi said, "A fish living in the ocean asked its friends, 'Where's the ocean. I've heard of it, but I've never seen it.' The friends took the fish to the edge of an underwater canyon and said, 'Do you see the dark waters there, that's the ocean.'"

Travis smiled. "The fish don't realize they're in the ocean."

Rishi shook his finger. "The ocean isn't just around the fish, the fish itself is part of the ocean. The ocean is not just the water, but everything animate and inanimate is included. The fish and the ocean are one. They are both ocean!" said Rishi.

"We are the Universe," said Travis. "The universe and we are one."

Rishi closed his eyes to experience stillness. "We're part of God. To look for God is silly, we're an integral part of the God-ocean." Rishi touched his arm. "No matter how imperfect people may think I am, no matter how hard they try, no one can take the Universe out of me. In every element of me, is God!"

"Wow!" Travis's faced glowed.

Rishi took his ring and let it roll gently on the coffee table. "This ring is gold. It's not all the gold on Earth. But no one can deny this ring its gold-ness. It will, forever, remain gold. We are the Universe. I'm not all the God that exists, but I am in my smallest way absolutely God."

"No one can deny us our God-ness. This is A-plus, Rishi, absolutely A-plus!" said Travis. "God and I are one!"

"We look for God all our lives without realizing who we truly are," said Rishi. "The flame searches for fire, not realizing it is fire itself. The wave searches for the ocean not realizing it is the ocean itself. The ocean is the essence, the core ingredient from which the waves rises and submerges back. The wave and the ocean are one, while the wave is in existence, and forever thereafter."

"Simple and deep." Travis took a deep breath.

A vibration went down Rishi's spine. With a rich voice, he said, "I've been saying we must experience our soul, the Truth is we are the soul, we need to experience our own self. The wave has to realize it is water, the shape of the wave is not the Truth because it is temporary, water is the Truth. The body is a temporary form, we are the soul. Our soul is God energy. Our body is God matter. God is the element, God is the core ingredient in Man, God is the divine energy in man. Man and God are one, while man is in existence, and forever thereafter. You cannot separate man from God, no more than can you separate flame from fire."

"I am God. You are God," said Travis.

"I am. You are!" said Rishi. They both hugged each other. Flame met flame, but fire remained unchanged. Wave hugged wave, but the ocean remained unchanged. Man hugged man, pervaded by the all-encompassing Universe.

As Travis took his seat he asked what he had asked at the beginning of the day, "I wish the Universe grants me peace."

"You don't have to ask for something you already have."

Travis looked amused.

"Yes, we all are peace at our very core. No one can take it from us, no one can give us peace. The Universe can't give us what we are already. We are peace! All we have to do is — be at peace. Be peace!"

"Be peace!" said Travis.

"Yes, be peace. God is peace. Peace is God. Meditate so you can be who you are. Be your essence. Be peace."

> *God is Peace!*
>
> *Peace is God!*

"Be peace," Travis repeated again.

"Be at peace. In Sanskrit, the word for peace is shaanthi. There's a

> *Be your essence!*
>
> *Be Peace!*

muntruh: Shaanthi. Shaanthi. Shaanthi."

"Shaanthi, shaanthi, shaanthi," said Travis.

Then neither said anything. Rishi closed his eyes to feel the stillness. The whole creation had stopped in its tracks.

After a few moments, Rishi stood up and extended his hand. Travis shook his hand, and then stretched his arms for a hug. Both embraced, needing each other's support, reassurance, and encouragement. They embraced for a long time.

Then Rishi stepped back from the embrace and pressed his right thumb gently against the space between Travis's eyebrows. Travis closed his eyes and became still. Rishi held his thumb in position for about sixty seconds. He then slightly pressed on the top of Travis's head and asked him to take three deep breaths. Rishi stepped back and stood there with his gaze on Travis.

Travis sat down, and closed his eyes for a couple of minutes, breathing deeply and slowly. He opened his eyes to see Rishi standing a few steps away, observing him. Rishi gestured with his palms open and turned upwards.

Travis extended his palms. Rishi stepped forward and gently pressed the center of Travis's right palm, and then his left palm. Touching Travis on the forehead and on the palms, Rishi felt he had connected the divine energies.

Rishi sat back on his sofa. "When the day started I thought I was the one helping you." Rishi pressed his palms against his chest. "Now, I realize, your coming here today has benefitted me deeply. It has served as a huge reminder to reduce my ego, and motivated me to push forward diligently with consistent effort." Rishi took a deep breath. Then, under his breath, Rishi recited, "Shaanthi, shaanthi… shaaaanthi."

Before Travis could say anything, Rishi closed his eyes. Travis felt immense peace emanating from Rishi. Travis closed his eyes and felt a deep sense of calm and relief.

The Universe had found its rhythm, or at a minimum, Rishi had synchronized his rhythm with the Universe. He felt as if the beginning of the end of his journey had arrived.

God is the Universe!

The Universe is God!

We are a part of the Universe.

We are a part of God.

Our body is a temporary form, like a wave.

For a wave, water is the permanent Truth,

similarly for us, the divine Soul is the

permanent Truth.

Chapter 21: Be Peace

For most of us, our river of life is caught in a pond. There is a lot of movement circling within the pond, but in the greater scheme, our lives are stagnant with no forward movement.

The infinite ocean awaits us. It beckons us, and most wonderfully, the Universe has gifted us the vehicle of spirituality to lead us naturally to the infinite.

Spiritual gravity acts on us constantly, but we must break through our obsessions and addictions with the material world to make the journey to our inner self.

Many people are spurred to act because of a catalyst whether it is a person, an event, or a crisis. That is great, but why wait? Experience the ocean of bliss within you. Do not miss out. Do not delay. Start the journey today.

Quiet your hungry mind, let your happy soul shine.
Be peace!
Meditate, meditate, meditate!! Peace, peace, p e a c e . . .

You are Peace!

Be who you are!

Be Peace!

Appendix

Spiritual Poem

Thought-free

A thought about you or me — is still a thought

A thought about good or bad — is still a thought

A thought about dreams or nightmares — is still a thought

A thought about love or hate — is still a thought

A thought about loved ones — is still a thought

A thought about the past, present, or the future — is still a thought

A thought about success or failure — is still a thought

A thought about awakening and living — is still a thought

A thought about sleeping and dying — is still a thought

A thought about possessing or renouncing — is still a thought

A thought about God or Anti-God — is still a thought

A thought about self-awareness — is still a thought

A thought about union with God — is still a thought

A thought about being peaceful — is still a thought

A thought about having no thoughts — is still a thought

Watching your own silent awareness — is still a thought

Do not watch your awareness, be one with your awareness

Be still, be thought…less, be thought-free

Be Thought-free. Be Nothingness.

You are Peace! Be your true self — Be Peace!

Peace… Peace… Peace…

Spiritual Chart

"Quiet your hungry mind, let your happy soul shine!"

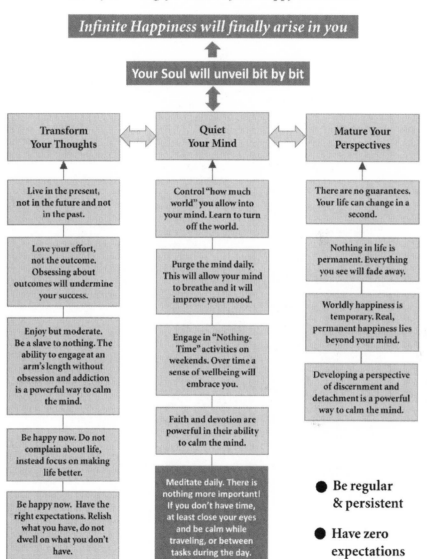

Infinite Happiness will finally arise in you

Your Soul will unveil bit by bit

Transform Your Thoughts	Quiet Your Mind	Mature Your Perspectives

Live in the present, not in the future and not in the past.

Control "how much world" you allow into your mind. Learn to turn off the world.

There are no guarantees. Your life can change in a second.

Love your effort, not the outcome. Obsessing about outcomes will undermine your success.

Purge the mind daily. This will allow your mind to breathe and it will improve your mood.

Nothing in life is permanent. Everything you see will fade away.

Enjoy but moderate. Be a slave to nothing. The ability to engage at an arm's length without obsession and addiction is a powerful way to calm the mind.

Engage in "Nothing-Time" activities on weekends. Over time a sense of wellbeing will embrace you.

Worldly happiness is temporary. Real, permanent happiness lies beyond your mind.

Be happy now. Do not complain about life, instead focus on making life better.

Faith and devotion are powerful in their ability to calm the mind.

Developing a perspective of discernment and detachment is a powerful way to calm the mind.

Be happy now. Have the right expectations. Relish what you have, do not dwell on what you don't have.

Meditate daily. There is nothing more important! If you don't have time, at least close your eyes and be calm while traveling, or between tasks during the day.

● Be regular & persistent

● Have zero expectations

Make the choice to be "happy" every day, even during difficult times.

© Ravi Kathuria

Spiritual Spiral

Spiritual Path

*"Quiet your hungry mind,
let your happy soul shine!"*

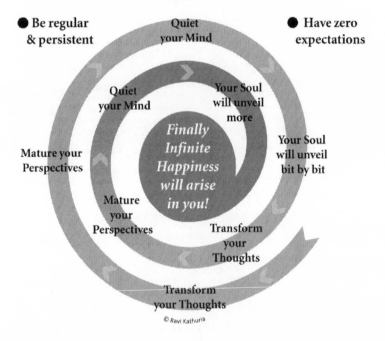

● Be regular
& persistent

Quiet
your Mind

● Have zero
expectations

Quiet
your Mind

Your Soul
will unveil
more

*Finally
Infinite
Happiness
will arise
in you!*

Your Soul
will unveil
bit by bit

Mature your
Perspectives

Mature
your
Perspectives

Transform
your
Thoughts

Transform
your Thoughts

© Ravi Kathuria

Acknowledgments

I pay homage to and thank all the gurus from whom I have garnered spiritual knowledge.

My Dad is my guru. He was a true seeker and philosopher, and deeply investigated the highest philosophical questions. I watched him meditate, and through his spiritual guru I was introduced to ancient Indian philosophy.

My mother taught me as a kid to be kind and gentle. I am still learning to be kinder and gentler. My mother, Dropadi, brother, Dilip, and sister, Sangeetha, in their spiritual quests have been great reminders for me to stay on the path.

I could not accomplish what I wanted to without the support of my wife, Seema. She has let me pursue what I desired unencumbered. She has been then there all along, unquestioning and unrelenting. It is the peace that she has brought in our household that has given me the freedom and courage to do what I was compelled to do.

Our sons, Amrit and Aayush have contributed to this work. Amrit has been such a great sounding board, as I flip-flopped between names for the book, and as I designed the diagrams that went along. He is wise and has a sense for aesthetics as well as an understanding of the message behind the graphic.

Aayush has a keen sense. He has effortlessly pointed out at times the most meaningful and yet obvious aspects I have missed or overlooked. His guidance at times has been eye-opening.

Several friends provided feedback on the book and their feedback was extremely valuable in improving the book. I acknowledge their help but more importantly their friendship. I want to thank BJ Farmer. He discussed the book in great detail with me, and I appreciated his robust pushbacks. His feedback was directly relevant and quite helpful. Daniel Magill went through the book with a fine comb, which was of great help. Bryant Price, Todd Frank, Alex Wolansky, Ronni Beyer, Dennis Tardan, Amit Dhawan, Sunil Jhangiani, Francisco Parra, and Eric Young, I thank them all for their help and valuable feedback.

I thank the Universe. I am just the conduit, the messenger. The words and messages are directly from the Universe. The words in the book have truly benefited me as the recipient. I am eternally grateful to the Universe for them.

Most of all, I am grateful to the Universe for giving us human beings the ultimate gift of spirituality!

About the Author

Ravi Gopaldas Kathuria

Ravi Kathuria is a student of
spirituality, a lifelong seeker.

Spiritual advancement is his
primary and ultimate purpose
in life. All he cares about is realizing the Truth and sharing the
Truth.

Connecting

For blogs and videos, to provide feedback and comments, and to connect with the author please visit:

www.HappySoulHungryMind.com

Made in the USA
Middletown, DE
10 December 2018